joy.ology

joy.ology

THE CHEMISTRY OF HAPPINESS

Turker Bas, PhD

TALENTE

TALENTE

First Edition
All rights reserved. Copyright © 2017 by Turker Bas, PhD

www.joyology.net

USA I Canada I UK I Germany I Turkey I India I China

The Business Centre 61 Wellfield Road 27 Colmore Row Birmingham England

Edition: Kerime Dalyan
Translation: Kerime Dalyan

Cover Design: M.Volkan Tarsus
Cartooning: Emirhan Perker

Talente also publishes its books in a variety of electronic formats and by print-on-demand. Some material included with standard print versions of this book may not be included in e-books or in print-on-demand.

Includes bibliographical references and index.

ISBN: 978-1-973-36534-1

1. Happiness 2. Neuroscience 3. Trust 4. Health I.Title

This book is dedicated to my late wife Ebru Baş (1976-2017).

Contents

Foreword

Confession time. All my life, I have been struggling for more happiness. Although my target in life seemed to be power, fame and status, my "happiness" was the real motive behind my continuous pursuit of success and career achievements. I thought they would make me a happier person. But, I was wrong. First off, success didn't make me happy at all. I imagined that doubling my income would take me to another level. It didn't. Also, the joy of achievement didn't last long. Accomplishing goals set ten years before didn't make me happier. In fact, I missed the life I had before my achievements. Those were perhaps the happiest days of my life and I didn't even realize it.

Then I noticed that I wasn't the only one going through this. My friends, colleagues and clients seemed to struggle with similar problems. They appeared successful, but, like me, couldn't find the inner peace and happiness they craved. Even the alpha males and females at the top of the food chain were not left out. Many CEOs experienced the same frustration. For instance, despite constant complaining about their busy schedules, they continued working after hours on auto-pilot. When on vacation, most of them were seldom more than two meters away from their cellphones or laptops and monitored office email traffic by the pool. Their relationships with family and friends were understandably strained.

Things were even more difficult for mid-level managers, especially for ambitious ones with challenging career goals. To these people, happiness was a luxury. Their mindset induced continuous hard work for promotion and created an anxious state of mind which distinguished them from other employees, but of course, not in a good way.

Lower level workers didn't get off lightly either. They were dissatisfied with their pay, work conditions and perks. Not to put too fine a point on it, almost everyone was feeling down in the dumps, no matter what level of the organization they came from.

I suppose this vicious cycle explains why I became so obsessed with studies of happiness and with questions such as,

- 'Why is unhappiness increasing?'
- 'Why do things we do for pleasure so often end in unhappiness?'
- 'How can we perpetuate our happiness?'

My inquisitiveness led me to research hundreds of articles and books on happiness, some decades old. It was hard going. Most of my research findings were contradictory and barely scratched the surface.

Some sources considered success as the major ingredient in happiness. Others claimed that a serene life style was the key to a happy life. Another group said we needed to raise our goals for finding happiness, while others urged us to lower them. To make matters worse, each group presented a valid argument in support of their case. Damn! This ambiguity wasn't very helpful to my research. In the end, I ditched the research entirely.

Then, a breakthrough. While rummaging through a book shop one day, I came across a yellowing book with the title, 'Truth and Lies About Why We Buy'. The book was underpinned by neurological research carried out by brand futurist, Martin Lindstrom.[1] His study cost seven million dollars and lasted three years. Lindstrom and his team studied buying instincts by monitoring brain activity using an advanced scanning technique known as fMRI (Functional Magnetic Resonance Imaging) which measured the amount of blood-oxygen mixture energizing the brain. This allowed Lindstrom to map the active parts of the brain. The results were striking. One study involving hundreds of people over six weeks, revealed that instead of invoking fear, health warnings on cigarette packs stimulated the desire region of the brain. Thus, anti-smoking campaigns that ran in a hundred and twenty countries and cost billions of dollars of tax payers' money, ended up motivating more people to smoke than quit. Wow that's a costly mistake.

These findings had parallels to my own research on happiness: That things we did to be happy were not only useless but escalated our misery even further. I was thrilled at the thought of bringing together happiness and neuroscience. Materials were abundant and readily available. I decided to apply Lindstrom's neuro-marketing approach to understand the dynamics of happiness. I discovered studies which explored how happiness formed in our brains, which chemicals made us happy and how these were triggered. There were enough studies on the subject to suggest a 'science of happiness'. This greatly improved my research.

On the other hand, I found scattered research results of studies conducted in labs and the usage of highly technical terms — known in the research world as boffin-speak —challenging, preventing me from arriving at a relevant conclusion. To overcome this, I began to research and observe people close to me. I tried to assess the neurologic principles that trigger happiness and describe what the equivalent of the laboratory results were in real life. Although neuroscience didn't give me all the answers I sought, it nevertheless provided a powerful framework for understanding the factors which made people happy and unhappy.

I extended my studies to companies where I worked as a consultant. I applied neuroscience principles and decided on what they wanted in their workplace. We carried out several projects using this approach. We restructured the working environment, performance, wage and bonus systems of the companies with this perspective. Almost all these projects were met with mixed feelings and resistance, however, they produced tremendous results in the long run.

The 'Joy.ology perspective', as I named it, was really working and it was time to share it with more people.

In summary, our thesis in this book is:

• We don't really know what makes us happy. And we remain unaware of the fact that often, the things we do to make us happy actually make us grumpier than a bear with toothache.

• Happiness and unhappiness are chemically created in the melting pot of our brains. Understanding the chemical basis for happiness is the way to achieve it.

• Such an understanding will help us become aware of alternatives that make us smile, laugh even. In addition, it will help us kick habits which make us unhappy way into the long grass.

Acknowledgments

I don't know how successful this book will be. What I do know is what made it possible in the first place — people. I couldn't feel luckier. Nor could I be more grateful to those — and there were many — who, in their own, unique ways, made this book possible. I particularly want to mention my family. I'm especially grateful for their unrelenting support over days, weeks and months of writing.

The book's content and arguments were noticeably sharpened by my son, Barensel's ceaseless questioning and manuscript suggestions. My mother, Hatice Bas and my brother Taner, are the recipients of my warmest gratitude for their unwavering trust.

I reserve my everlasting gratitude, however, for my sweet, beautiful wife and hero, Ebru, who shared my passion from the very first minute, and who, sadly, passed away earlier this year. Ebru had been an incredible resource and guide throughout the whole process, with her always encouraging, and loving approach. She was an irreplaceable source of deep, tenacious, truthful exchange on the many beauties of life. But above everything else, she had kept me full of life and enthusiasm for the past 20 years, every single day. Her love was a true reflection of God's unconditional love, and I will never be able to thank her enough for this blessing. She is terribly missed and this book is dedicated to her memory, with all my heart.

Elif Tugba Avşar is my great friend. She earns the first mention after my family, for her invaluable point of view, her unwavering interest in the subject of happiness and her brief in the concepts that make up the book. Kerime Dalyan proved to be more than a translator and editor. She challenged my hop-and-skip brain to stay focused and pushed me to make him understand what I was trying to communicate. Her translation is superb and his passion indispensable. I appreciate the sacrifice in time spent away from his beloved son, Ali. I am extremely grateful for the constant and professional proofreading support of George Anderson for his extraordinary eye for detail. Thanks too, to Volkan Tarsus, for designing the perfect book cover, for your creativity, and for helping to set up The Joy.ology Project. Emirhan Perker is one of the most creative persons I have ever met, and I will never be able to thank him enough for his fascinating cartoons.

Looking toward my friends, Yüksel Samast, Basar Akpinar, Ataman Ozbay, Baris Akpinar and Haluk Sicimoglu, were instrumental in getting the premise straight in my head (even if they didn't realize that that's what they were doing at the time). Great Place to Work Turkiye, General Manager Eyup Toprak proved vital as a sounding board and head-scratcher when certain ideas needed polishing. Mahmut Akbolat, along with his assistants at Sakarya University, were a constant source of help and support. A small group of wise colleagues read specific chapters for me and I'm indebted to them for their time and expert guidance: Berrin Tavman, Osman Unal, Can Saka, Ersel Oran. Many other researchers, too numerous to mention, helped me out by sending their journal articles, or answering my queries. I would like to express my deep gratitude to the clients and friends who agreed to share their stories, and to many others whose experiences were incorporated in short form to make these pages come alive. Hearty thanks go to all neuroscientists and experts I interviewed, for their generosity of time and assistance. Many thanks also to my doctoral students from Galatasaray University, for all shared efforts and great times spent building a forum for innovative discussions across the neuroscience of happiness. My assistant, Mustafa Amarat, has been invaluable - handling a multitude of issues that freed up the time I needed to devote to the book.

Finally, thank you to the participants of my joy.ology courses who have shared with me their glories, dramas, and dreams and who have enabled me to consider real sources of happiness!

Joy.ology: Overview

Truths We are Not Aware of

Let's start with four truths about "happiness" which make up the basis of our approach called Joy.ology:

1. We may believe we live for happiness but our brain only works towards survival and continuation of our species. Happy chemicals function to tell us "go on, you are on the right track" when we act in line with this purpose.

2. Our factory settings are not up-to-date. That's why it is difficult to be happy in modern life.

3. We deceive our brains. Namely, we have devised certain mechanisms to activate the happy chemicals for reasons other than survival.

4. Unhappiness is not a destiny. We can change as opposed to popular belief.

We were part of a group of hundreds. We have been traveling on a train for the last couple of days. The passengers looked like skeletons, their bodies barely covered by their skin and the rags they had on. Almost all their fat and muscles had been melted away. Yet, there was no place in the wagon, even to crouch. Most of us had to stand. The exhausted dozed off, leaning on those next to them.

The train slowed as we approach the station. Suddenly, the anxious passengers shouted in alarm, "There is a Mauthausen sign!". Hearts almost stopped beating on hearing this word, because it evokes the horror of the gas chambers, the crematoria where the bodies of the dead were burned, mass graves and so on. The train was slow, almost hesitant, as if it was trying to protect the passengers for as long as possible from the unbearable imagery which the sign conjures up. Tension amongst the passengers doubled as we near a bridge over the Danube. Those who recalled travelling this route before remembered it as a landmark on the way to Mauthausen. All passengers held their breath. Then the silence was shattered with a greater magnitude of joyful cries and an outbreak of dancing among the passengers as they realized that the train have been redirected to Dachau instead. In the hours that follow, we joked and laughed despite all we had been through.

When we reached the camp, the count indicated one person missing. We were made to wait in the rain, in the cold and windy weather, until he was found. The missing prisoner was apparently in one of the barracks where he had fallen asleep out of fatigue. The count became a show of punishment. We were held in bitter cold, all night and until late morning. Yet, we were still happy because we were not in Mauthausen.[1]

This terrifying story of Dr. Victor Frankl[2], reveals four truths about 'happiness' which are often ignored. These truths make up the basis of my approach which I call Joy.ology.

First Truth:
We are striving for survival, that's all

1.

It's hard to grasp what Dr. Victor Frankl had to go through when, with the exception of his sister, he lost his whole family in Germany's concentration camps. Can you even imagine the people from the story metamorphosing into skeletons, their muscles wasted by starvation? Can you picture them after a trip of two days packed like sardines, dancing on their own feces, joking and laughing? Moreover, their spirits never flagged even when kept up all night under the pouring rain.

How could these people in the concentration camps possibly be happy when crushed by so much cruelty and hunger, their values demolished, fearing death every moment while in our modern, wealthy society many people seem to have forgotten how to smile?

A decade ago such questions would have created serious confusion. Today, we can explain Dr. Frank's experience by reflecting on recent developments in the field of neuroscience.

2.

The latest experiments with advanced imaging technology have brought our conceptions about happiness right up to date. Now we know that happiness:

• Functions as the basic mechanism to compensate for the survival and continuation of mankind,[3]

• Results from the release of at least one of the brain chemicals, dopamine, serotonin, endorphin and oxytocin.[4]

You may believe you live for happiness but your brain works towards survival and the continuation of our species. Happy chemicals say 'go on, you're on the right track' when you act in line with this purpose.[5] Diverge from this purpose and you trigger the stress chemical cortisol — your brain's warning of the need for immediate, corrective action.[6]

Every chemical has a unique job to do. Dopamine, for example, is a stimulant which creates the sensation of accomplishment whenever we meet our goals and objectives.[7] The feeling of pride comes from serotonin, a chemical stimulated by the admiration and appreciation of others.[8] Endorphin — a natural morphine — masks physical pain.[9] It kicks in when we are injured or after challenging physical activity. Oxytocin enables us to trust others, making cooperation and association possible.[10]

Importantly, these reward mechanisms have evolved specifically to service the survival and continuation of mankind. That's why remaining idle for long periods makes you unhappy. And it offers an explanation why the super-rich continue to work long after they could just spend the rest of their lives counting their ill-gotten gains. Therefore our happy moments are short-lived. For example, we might put all our efforts over several years into gaining a much-desired promotion. When our promotion finally comes, we are floating on a magic carpet of happiness, thanks to chemicals that get awfully excited when good news comes along. However, within days all returns to normal. The promotion is achieved and the mission of happy chemicals is completed. Triggering them again may require renewed acclamations of our achievements. Moreover, the bigger the success, challenge or resolution, the higher the volume of happy chemicals released. This is why we try so hard to get attention and yearn for success.

3.

Going back to the fundamental question: How is it that joy could be experienced in the concentration camps while people in our modern, wealthy society find it difficult to smile?

Frankl suggests that, 'when people suddenly grasp they have nothing to lose but their lives, they are concerned only with keeping what is at hand and developing it. This is key to survival. Everything else is to be disregarded'.

Frankl and his friends struggled for survival in primitive conditions. Nothing else mattered save remaining alive. In the midst of this battle, the reward — that is to say the amount of happy chemicals produced is proportional to the magnitude of the danger escaped. As the train heads towards the concentration camp away from the danger of the gas chamber, the happy chemicals rushed into their blood, misery and hunger suppressed, overcome with joy, they all started dancing.

Second Truth:
Our factory settings are not up-to-date

4.

When I first read the research findings about how our brain rewards efforts which enhance the ability of our species to survive, I thought, surely, we're living in the happiest era in the history of mankind. After all, wild capitalism is parallel to wild nature in terms of brutality. In the modern world, we are constantly faced with the quest for survival. We set off to work early in the morning and return late in the day. In between times we are constantly engaged in struggling to make ends meet. So why, I thought, aren't we happy after all this?

5.

The human brain emerged approximately 2,5 million years ago. Then, when few people were around to witness it, it tripled in mass, reaching the 1,500 grams of the modern human brain from that of Homo Habilis' 560 grams. All this progress took place during the so-called 'hunter-gatherer' phase except for the last 10 thousand years after mankind settled.

Therefore, within this period, survival challenges and their respective resolutions have shaped the human brain. As a result, we are trying to find our way through the modern world's super complexity using a control system designed for the primitive era.[11]

Our out of date factory settings are the root cause of many of the problems we currently face — including unhappiness. However, unaware of this situation, we have become smug enough to believe that we have a perfect brain compared to other living creatures — a conviction that collapses like a failed soufflé under the lightest of scrutiny. Our fondness for sticking with our inbuilt conditioning, makes us fall, time and again, in the same pit.

During my research, I came across a rich seam of data about lottery billionaires — clearly a popular of subject. I discovered a regular pattern in the lives of these billionaires. The moment they are in the money, they chase after the life they've always dreamt of.[12] Naturally. In many cases the unbecoming demands of relatives and friends forced them to leave their familiar surroundings, break with their past and start a new life elsewhere. Surprise, surprise, they end up struggling to become a part of this new environment. Many are either defrauded or betrayed by their new friends and spouses.

Consequently, they exhaust their riches, ruin their social relations and end up worse off than when they started. It's a bleak thought, I know, but regardless of their country or culture, young or old, educated or not, they followed a similar downward spiral to unhappiness, with some making the same mistakes over and over again. As in the case of the guy who hit the jackpot 3 times and still ended up polishing shoes.[13]

The comments under the news and articles were even more interesting. The miserable lives and dead-end situations of the lottery winners appeared not to have affected one single reader. None of them showed any concern that similar riches might blight their future. They considered themselves special enough not to make such mistakes. 'If I win …' they'd say, before explaining in detail, how they would spend the money if they hit the jackpot. Interestingly, their plans were almost identical to those of the winners. In other words, they openly stated that they would repeat the same behaviours yet somehow these would lead, in their cases, to happy endings.[14]

Actually, mankind faces similar problems in modern life but the negative outcomes for the lottery winners are much deserved and evident since they chose to cut corners. For instance, most people choose their profession largely based on society's definition of success. I'll be-

21

come a lawyer they say, then end up working 100-hour weeks and having nervous breakdowns. Or a doctor, they cry, before working 72 hours straight on the ward, ending up unable to read a thermometer. Consequently, they end up miserable about what they do and regretting the choices they made.

As they forge ahead in their career, they are motivated and happy with what they do, placing their work over every other thing — family and friends included. However, as their dreams come within touching distance, the color drains out of their life and they start pining for the good old days. Nostalgia isn't what it used to be, as they say. They become aware that they no longer derive happiness in things that used to please them. They sense insincerity in people around them. Not good!

The desire of the lottery winner to chase his dreams, the drive for people to choose prestigious professions, struggling to climb the career ladder, and so on, are all normal steps to take to reach happiness. They all move forward with their factory settings intact, trying to find a way through the chaos of modern life with a system fit only for the purpose of survival in a primitive world. The result is that we constantly lose our way.

'This is who I am. This is my destiny,' they say in their defence when they reach deadlock. They deem their lives to have predetermined boundaries within which they have little power to bring about a positive change.

No need to drive ourselves off a cliff just yet, however. There is an alternative approach which can turn our lives around — an approach leading to sustainable happiness. And here I am certainly not thinking about the limited and incoherent strategies popular of late: 'Positive thinking', 'Think simple', or 'Awaken the sleeping potential within us.' What we really need is a paradigm shift, a receptive point of view that will enable us to go beyond conventional wisdom to provide real results. Essentially, we must understand our brains' factory settings, and the problems they cause.

Third Truth:
We deceive our brains

6.

When faced with danger or even unfavorable conditions, the primitive part of our brain —the cells in charge of our emotions — throws a hissy fit like Vivian Leigh in Gone with the Wind and triggers the production of cortisol, setting off our inner alarm system.[15] Our system prepares itself to stay and fight or run away — the classic 'Fight or Flight' response.[16] That's all very well when the chances of a T.Rex decapitating you as you left your cave for a pee in the morning were as high as rain on Borneo, that's all well and good. But to throw a primeval hissy fit because you have locked yourself out of your car? That's overkill. Cortisol floods the bloodstream like a river in spate. The rational centers of the brain begin to generate alternative solutions to the problem at hand. Often, these alternatives are pretty clear. For instance, we eat when we are hungry. We leave a building that is on fire. We run away from a dog that is about to attack us. Our brains easily find solutions to problems mankind has faced for millions of years.

Fine. But the problems of the modern world are not so simple. For example, when a two-hour delay to our flight is announced, our primitive brain can't help itself. It releases cortisol signaling a message to our rational brain: 'Do something! But, in this case, the rational brain has no answers. Yet the primitive brain keeps on producing cortisol and grows ever more insistent that a resolution must be found: "Don't just stand there! Do something! Do something! Do something!".

But, good news — depending on the situation, a piece of chocolate or a hot dog is sufficient to get the primitive mind to chill out. The primitive brain, overwhelmed by such a high calorie explosion not readily available off a nearby bush, releases a high volume of dopamine which in turn reduces cortisol concentration, thereby making us feel better. That is why many people overeat when stressed. Besides, the more calories we consume, the more dopamine is released. This explains why we can't overcome stress by nibbling broccoli or leeks. Luckily for us, we have pizza and French fries to help![17]

7.

During paleolithic ages the amount of calories consumed by our ancestors had to be equivalent or more than the calories burned during the hunting. The primitive brain enabled mankind to proritize among naturally available food via rewarding high calorie with more dopamine, a phenomenon still common among all mammals except human beings.[18] Mankind have achieved superiority over other living things by improving methods and arms for hunting. This provided him with more dopamine, meaning more happiness from less effort. A "great success" was recorded from the Neolithic age, when mankind has been able to produce crop and his struggle with nature has been in his favor. Our ancestors no longer ate to survive, but rather survived to eat. This change in life's purpose has resulted in nutritional disorders such as obesity and epidemic, life expentancy dropped to 20 years from 33 years and could not reach its early level for approximately 10 thousand years.[19] Though our ancestors, for ages, lead a more comfortable life but lived less. So, if you've been a tad overenthusiastic at the 'All you can eat for $5 buffet', blame your Neolithic cousins.

Certainly, this deceit was not limited to the abundance of food.[20] Mankind, over time, discovered alcohol, opium and tobacco. Games to trigger happy chemicals followed suit. The primitive brain[21] rewarded game victories in a similar manner to our struggle to survive.[22] Then, we have noticed that our primitive brain was reacting to others' experiences as it was his own which led to the development of fine arts such as literature, theatre and cinema. Mankind has started to rejoice or saddened with others 'stories, shared their happiness and pain.[23]

In summary, by tricking our primitive brains, we have devised certain mechanisms to activate the happy chemicals for reasons other than survival. This has enriched our lives but on the other hand has brought along risks of dragging us to unhappiness. Hence, our happiness depends on managing these risks involved. To this end, we are in need of a thorough understanding of our brain and how the happy chemicals function.

Fourth Truth:
We can change as opposed to popular belief

8.

One day, back when scorpions and frogs could speak each other's languages, a scorpion asked a frog who was lying in the sun by a river to help him cross to the other side. 'Does it look like my head zips up the back,' the frog said, 'You will sting me', and rejected the scorpion's call for help. The scorpion said "No, that will drown both of us". Thinking about it for a minute, the frog agreed with him. And so, the frog took the scorpion on his back and started swimming towards the shore. When they reached the middle of the river, the scorpion stung the frog on the back of his neck. The frog's body turned cold and immediately his legs and feet felt numb. At his last breath, about to sink completely, the frog asked, 'Now why on earth did you have to do that?' The scorpion's response was simple: 'What can I do? This is my nature.'

Almost everybody in the business world has had to listen to this tale more than once. Most managers are comfortable telling this tale, although the rest of us are bored rigid by it, because it attempts to blame the inadequate parenting skills of Mother Nature, instead of taking responsibility for the often-unpalatable results of their own tough decisions. As an example, when you question their short temper, they'll say, 'There isn't much I can do about this, it's in my nature'. Actually, this is in partly true since it has been scientifically proven in genetic determinism that, to a large extent; human behavior is determined by our genes.[24]

The first question that springs to mind might be, 'Why are some managers more humane than others?' 'How can such a difference come about despite genetic determinism?' The answer to this has been given by Freud's theory of psychic determinism which states that our nature is shaped by our childhood experience and upbringing.[25] For instance, if we cannot speak in public, this is because of our parents, there is nothing we can do about it, it is how we were brought up.

In conclusion, until recently, the prevailing scientific attempts to explain human behavior were genetic determinism and psychic determinism. That is to say, we come to this world with our genetic heritage. Besides, life experiences affect the development of our brain, shaping our character and personal tendencies. So, if you're an axe murderer, you have the perfect alibi. This approach has given us the right to blame our genes, family or ancestors instead of taking responsibility for our actions. However, recent progress in the field of neuroscience draws a clearer picture.[26] From now on we know we can change. There is no longer any excuse to lay blame elsewhere. We just need to take the necessary steps.

PART ONE

Who has the control?

Descartes' Error

Happiness is in great demand. People want it a lot. Yet there never seems to be enough of it to go around. The situation is tense. Important questions on the subject go unanswered! Questions like, 'Why does happiness have such a short shelf life?' and 'Why can't we just make the decisions we know would make us happy? You might reasonably expect to find answers to these elusive questions between the covers of the many personal development books that nowadays crowd our bookshop shelves. Yet this is not the case. If only happiness were available on prescription!

By the time, you reach the end of this introductory chapter I cannot guarantee you will have found happiness but I'm sure you'll have a much better understanding of how our brain works by going beyond the conscious mind and how this opens innovative pathways to personal happiness.

The silent morning was interrupted by an untimely phone call. This call was actually the start of a series of events that made Canan Karatay, the world-renowned cardiology professor, the top news story and household name.[1] The phone stopped ringing just as Doctor Karatay, totally clueless as to what was about to befall her, reached the phone. "It must be a wrong number", she said to herself. As she turned to leave the room, the phone started to ring again. This time she reached for the phone hesitantly, sensing that something was in store for her. Her anxiety and concern could be heard in her voice. "Hello," she said.

The person on the phone introduced himself as Superintendent Mehmet. Doctor Karatay, at 74, was astonished. This was the first time she had ever been called by the police. The name "Mehmet" gave her a sense of relief; it was her son's name, providing a bit of warmth and trust for the caller. Yet, this was not going to last long.

"Yes officer – is there a problem?" asked Doctor Karatay.

"Doctor Karatay, we have found your credentials on a PKK[1] terrorist who died during a tactical operation. We have traced two separate accounts in your name, one in Switzerland and one in Kuwait."

Doctor Karatay's astonishment turned into shock. Her name being associated with a terrorist organization was mind numbing. She felt tension in every single muscle in her body, as her heart began to

---

[1] The PKK, also known as KADEK, is internationally listed as a terrorist organization by several states and organizations, including the North Atlantic Treaty Organisation (NATO), the United States, and the European Union (EU).

pound in her chest. A short shiver followed, her body chemistry was completely unsettled.

Without a pause, the accusations followed one after the other, hardly letting her catch a breath. "We have detected a transfer of three hundred and eighty thousand US dollars to Switzerland from your account in Kuwait. Our operation is still in progress. We don't think you have committed a crime but you are a suspect nevertheless."

Doctor Karatay was profoundly affected by this stream of accusations. Her inner voice told her that none of this could be true. It had to be a mistake. But she could not pull herself together enough to question what was happening.

"Alright, but what can I do?" she asked.

"I will put you through to our prosecutor. But before I do, just be aware, he lost his nephew last week in an anti-terrorist operation. He's going through a very difficult period, so please be aware of this in your conversation with him," Superintendent Mehmet said.

Doctor Karatay was trying to make some sense out of the humming noise and the sound of the wireless in the background which was accompanied by shouts and swearing. Obviously, it was extremely busy at the police station. She was getting more and more nervous and was just beginning to think of ways to get out of the situation when she heard a voice on the line.

"Doctor Karatay, this is prosecutor Mustafa." His voice did not have an official or threatening tone. Rather, it was sad and sounded quite helpful. She relaxed slightly and felt a little closer to the prosecutor.

"Yes, Mister Prosecutor"

"We have started nationwide operations simultaneously in 14 cities across Turkey. We are expecting that you will cooparate with us for the sake of your country. You cannot say anything about this to anyone not even those closest to you. You have to be extremely careful because they have spies everywhere. The smallest mistake can ruin the whole operation, and you don't want to be responsible for that, do you?"

"Of course, Mister Prosecutor, I am ready to do all I can." A ray of hope appeared within her. She could certainly feel a sense of relief.

"Alright then Doctor Karatay, let's start. Superintendent Mehmet will explain what you have to do, step by step. Meanwhile, your mobile has to be switched on at all times. We must be able contact you all at any time. This is extremely critical."

Mehmet stepped in. He was now dictating, and sounded very firm.

"Based on the information we have, today there will be a money transfer from your bank accounts in Istanbul to a PKK account in Diyarbakır. You will have to go to the bank in order to prevent this transfer. We are going to use your money to stop the fraud and tomorrow we will put the money back into your bank account. In addition, you will be safe under our witness protection program. Now, there is no time to lose. You must leave your house for the bank immediately. From now on, we will be liaising through mobiles. Now, can I have your mobile number please?"

Doctor Karatay gave her number without hesitation. Her mobile rang immediately after. Once again it was superintendent Mehmet on the phone, talking too fast.

"I hope your battery is fully charged because from this moment on you must not switch off your phone, no matter what. Your phone must be on at all times, even if it is in your bag or pocket. This is very important."

"Okay. I will not switch my phone off. It will be on at all times." For a moment, the thought crossed her mind, "What if I fail and end up with all these accusations?" She took a few deep breaths and dismissed the thought. "You can do this", she told herself, just trust these officers and follow their instructions.

On that day, Doctor Karatay followed the instructions of a criminal who had introduced himself as Superintendent Mehmet. She withdrew twenty thousand US dollars and forty thousand Turkish Liras from two banks, and left it in two different locations, as per his instructions. Without saying a word to anyone, she then returned home and waited for her husband to arrive home. She was profoundly affected by what had occurred.

Doctor Karatay's experience is not an isolated case. According to police records, between October 2013 and April 2014, 656 people have been defrauded in a similar way. Most were very well educated.

For instance, criminal lawyer Professor Erdener Yurtcan left two and a half million Turkish Liras at a bus station[2] and Professor Halit Demir placed one hundred and seventy-three thousand Turkish Liras in a dustbin.[3] Psychologist Elvin Aydın did not have sufficient cash, so she placed her jewelry in a bag and left it in a park.[4] There have even been cases where people have taken out bank loans in order to provide the money.[5]

How could these influential people, who have inspired others with books and speeches, have been so easily duped? How could they believe such a simple story? How could they ever put their life savings in a bag and leave it on a pavement or in a park?

Let's have a look deep into our minds to see what is going on before we answer these questions.

1.

If we were to liken the human brain to an onion consisting of layers, the middle part would represent "primitive structures" left from first ages. Reflex actions such as breathing, smiling and screaming are largely governed by these structures. This part of our brain carries out these activities based on genetic codes that have developed over millions of years.[6] Over time, we add new skills or activities such as speaking, cycling and playing a musical instrument. These activities are not deliberate and they require little or no mental effort. From now on we will call these early structures as "Primitive Brain".

The recent "add-ons" are situated on the outer parts of our brain, close to our skull. The relatively new structures, which we call the "Rational Brain", comes into play when we are faced with complicated activities such as calculating, which is not stored in the archives of our primitive brain. For instance, driving on an empty road does not require a deliberate effort. We can perform this activity with the genetic codes of our primitive brain. However, when we are in heavy traffic or in an unknown area we resort to the guidance of our rational brain. Similarly, our primitive brain automatically calculates 2x2 whereas the rational brain comes to the rescue for a more complex operation like 23x17. Activities that are governed by the rational brain require effort and attention, and they tend to falter when distracted.[7]

2.

Now, I would like you to picture everything you do after you wake up in the morning. You get out of bed, put on a gown, and check your mobile phone while you are walking to the kitchen. You start the coffee machine and go to the bathroom for a shower. After the shower, you turn on the TV and watch the news while you are having your coffee. Then, you brush your teeth, dress and leave the house. I might have skipped some details but what we do in the mornings is pretty much the same every day. As a matter of fact, everything is somewhat standard, including the amount of tooth paste we use, and the coffee we drink. We repeat routines at the office, during our lunch breaks and after we get home. Thus, a considerable part of our lives is managed by the primitive part, deep in our brain.

On the other side, the rational brain has very limited access to what's going on. That is the reason we are unaware of what takes place behind many of our simplest activities. For example, in order to turn the pages of this book that you are reading right now, thousands of muscles and tendons have to move at a specific angle, with a specific amount of force, and in a synchronized manner. Our primitive brain produces separate signals for each and every one of these based on its previous learning. Thanks to this, we are able to caress a puppy, stop our car safely, and read a book without tearing the pages.[8]

We prefer to identify ourselves with the rational brain, when in fact our primitive brain runs the show for 95% of our lives. We glorify the rational brain's capacity to think, analyze and make decisions, and we brag about these abilities. As for the primitive brain, we view it as a loyal servant doing all the grunt work. We assume that the primitive brain moves within the confines set by the rational brain and follows the master's orders. We enjoy things being orchestrated at the back stage with the assumption that we are in control and can interfere wherever we want.

If our primitive brain is merely involved with various chores and does not move beyond boundaries drawn by the rational brain, then, why can't people give up their bad habits, even though they are aware of the harm? Why can't they make radical changes in their lives? Why can't they keep away from high-calorie food or continue with their workouts? If we go back to Doctor Karatay's case, why would anyone leave all their savings in a rubbish bin after being threatened over the phone? Now let's answer these questions with scientific research and experiments.

3.

In an experiment at the Houston Baylor College of Medicine, participants were asked to choose between two beverages, with the brand names concealed.[9] As you might guess, one of the drinks was Coca Cola and the other was Pepsi. More than half of the participants preferred Pepsi without knowing the brand. When asked about their preference criterion, without exception they said "taste". The experiment was repeated the next day, this time with brand names revealed. Participants tasted both beverages again and made their decisions but something seemed to be wrong. Every two out of three-people changed their choice and went for Coca-Cola, thus increasing its rate of preference from 40% to 70%. Did perception of taste change when the brand names were revealed? Or was it something else?

Fortunately, in both experiments, the respondents' brains were observed via MRI scans, which recorded how the choice came about and how the brain functioned. In the first experiment, researchers observed intense activity in part of the brain that is responsible for "taste" which showed that people really made their choice, as claimed, based on a careful comparison of the two drinks. Yet, in the second part of the experiment, in which the brand names were revealed, researchers detected a rush of blood to the "emotional" part of the brain, as well as the part that deals with "taste." The logos, design, brand history and advertising images all came into play. This indicates a silent internal clash of the rational brain and the primitive brain.

Result: The winner of the challenge was the primitive brain, as usual. Participants changed their choices; taste as a preference factor had almost disappeared. However, the rational brain rejecting defeat, as it always has, produced excuses such as, "I like Coca Cola's taste anyway" to rationalize the situation.

So what is the reason for such behavior? Why do we let our primitive brain govern us instead of us taking charge? Can it be due to the lack of awareness or effort? Absolutely, no! Don't blame yourself for this.

The problem stems from technical reasons. *The rational brain does not possess sufficient capacity and competence to govern.*

4.

My wife is doing dinner, listening to her friend's problems over the phone, taking care of the kids and listening to the news on TV. Yet she manages to do all these in a perfect harmony. She can respond if she is asked what was her friend's last words or can summarize the most important news headlines.

I know you are not impressed because we experience similar things every day and some would claim to be able to do even more. Interestingly, we don't even notice what a great job we do when we carry out all these activities simultaneously. While our rational brain brags about solving the simplest problems, our primitive brain processes a pile of information quietly.

Do you think this is an exaggeration? Then, let's build up a special scenario that would put our rational brain into action. Let's ask my wife to weigh each ingredient and add it to the meal at predetermined timings. For example, let's create a job flow that instructs her to add 170 gm. of onion, 150 gm. of pepper at 8th minute, 220 gm. tomatoes at the 13th minute and 400 gm. of meat at the 21st minute into the pan. Initially, one might consider such a plan would minimize mistakes. Yet, my wife would not be fond of this at all because with this method, she will have to close the phone, turn off the TV and isolate herself in the kitchen from the rest of the world to be able to pay attention to all the details. Hence, forced consciousness distrupts our simultaneous activities and results in a serious decline in capacity.

Will a single focus bring better results? "Yes", if you are a beginner, or in other words, didn't develop the relevant templates in your brain yet. However, imposing such a method on an experienced cook would just reduce him/her to an average one. Basketball players experience this dilemma during free throws. Majority of high performing players miss the throws during a game and end up performing below average because of too much attention placed on them. If you are playing a musical instrument, the moment you start focusing on your fingers, your performance drops rapidly. A millipede was asked "how do you manage to walk?" and from that moment, he couldn't take even one more single step further. Just like millipedes, when we think too much about the activity at hand, we end up failing at it. It becomes hard to perform things we function at perfectly.

5.

The performance of the primitive brain varies according to what had been stored over time. Whereas the rational brain produces a special resolution for every single incident, primitive brain reacts to situations based on readily available information in its archives. Therefore, if you are not happy with your own reaction to a specific event, this might result from these two reasons:

1. The information in the archive is not correct.
2. No such information exists in the archive.

A perfect illustration for the former is Mary's story; she had a severe accident after a night out.[18] The young girl was in a deep state of shock and cannot remember or recall any scene from the accident. She recovered in a while and was discharged from the hospital. One day, she suddenly had a panic attack at the campus café and this went on for several times. Her friends immediately shared this observation with school therapist. The therapist helped Mary in recalling what happened at the night of the accident. It turned out that her friends were laughing at the back seat when the accident happened. Mary's primitive brain associated laughter with the accident. Despite the knowledge that there is no correlation whatsoever, she can't prevent her primitive brain from thinking so.

Actually, the situation of people who panic or over react to criticisms is not so different to Mary's case. They are quite aware of the aftermath of their behavior, yet they fail to resist and function within the behavioral templates of their primitive brain's archives.

What if there is nothing to process or react towards? Do we remain unresponsive or alternatively scan our archives for a similar incident, choose and react accordingly?

Now, imagine yourself driving on a summer day. Suddenly, a giant bee enters the car from the open window. What would you do?

(a) Pull the car over immediately and give the unwanted guest a warm hospitality.

(b) Try to chase off and get rid of the bee.

I don't know what your answer would be, but the insurance data indicates an average of 650,000 car and motorcycle accidents per year. So, every year, hundreds of thousand s of people are engaged in an auto-crash while sending off a bee. They would all admit to the foolishness of their reaction yet can't avoid it. Again, insurance companies' records reveal that the rate of recurrent accident because of a bee is 1 out of 100,000, this is a reduction from the first case. That is to say, the primitive brain updates its archives and learns how to respond in the correct manner after a bitter experiment.[19]

Going back to Dr. Karatay's story, one would initially think, "Even a primary school leaver would understand the set up and not fall into such trap." What we have learned so far does not make us a neuroscience expert; however, it helps us to comprehend the unfairness and the irrelevance of this criticism. Now, we at least understand:

• IQ or education levels are indications of how developed the rational brain is.

• With the disengagement of the rational brains at the times of stress, all previleges acquired by education lose their significance.

One morning, you wake up and receive a phone call being accused of your involvement with a terrorist group, if such a thing hasn't happened to you before or is not registered in your brain, you would freak out, even having the IQ level of Einstein would not save you. You would do anything possible to offer any amount just to rule you out of such just like Doctor Karatay and hundreds of smart and well-educated people did.

6.

Interestingly, all these comparisons remind me of kings who accede the throne at a very young age. Especially the relationship between the French King, Louis XIV and Cardinal Jules Mazarin is an epitome of what goes on in our brains.[20]

Louis XIV was a child when he became the king after his father Louis XIII died of tuberculosis. France had the brightest period during his reign, thanks to Cardinal Jules Mazarin in the back stage. Louis was all about ambition and pride, he recognized no other authority which has always reflected in his words; "I am the state". Mazarin was a man of clergy with vast political experience. He let Louis own all the successes, never went into the spotlight. On the other hand, Louis proved to be a fast learner and astonished Mazarin with his astuteness. But still, he was a child. He was so obsessed with power yet hated bureaucracy. He delegated all to Mazarin, even the things he had to handle himself. Especially, in the shady and risky periods, he would lock himself in his room till the danger is gone. On the other hand, Mazarin had extensive experience enabling him to govern various matters at a given time. But he was a very conservative and religious man; inflexible, lacking tolerance towards different ideas. His approach ensured speed and consistency yet caused him to stumble and get confused against new problems.

It will give a clearer picture of what goes in our heads, if we imagine Louis as the rationale brain and Mazarin as the primitive brain. Rational brain with a history of just a few hundreds of thousands of years, is inexperienced compared to the primitive brain with a reservoir of millions of years' genetic evolutionary history just like Louis. And again, the it is as ambitious and as proud as Louis. It deems itself to be the ultimate master of neural system. Yet, all is orchestrated at the background by Mazarin, namely primitive brain.

7.

Several questions listed before I started working on "happiness" will be restated here just to refresh your minds. Some of which might seem contradictory or hit brick wall in your mind. Here are the questions that form the starting points of this book:

How on earth can people who hardly feed themselves purchase luxury goods? Why are some people hooked with gambling and are addicted to casinos? Why do we start worrying when our kids are only a few minutes late? Why are we unable to sleep when our boss disproves us? Why do we get into heated quarrels with people when in traffic? Why do we keep shopping even with the degree of our debts? Why can't we stay clear of high calorie food? Why can't we stick to diets that will improve our health and help as look better? Why do we ignore the benefits of exercise? Why do we fail to put a distance between ourselves and things which will definitely make us miserable in the long run? Why do Hollywood stars with such glamour end their own lives?

There is a general answer to all of these questions, an answer we don't want to admit to and find difficult just to be true to ourselves.[21] We don't put our thoughts into practice, we don't keep our own self-promises and we do things we later regret because; WE AREN'T IN CONTROL!

In summary, our happiness is not governed by the rational brain but rather the mechanisms deep in our brains, that is to say the primitive brain runs the show. From the previous example, happiness of France was in the hands of Cardinal Mazarin, not Louis who was just a kid. But until now, all our focuse was on Louis, our rational brain. We have read books and take education in order to develop our rational side. Our basic assumption is; the more we know or the more information we have, the better decisions we make. Yet, our choices do not meet our expectations in terms of happiness and when they do, it's only for a short period. Moreover, in the long run, we end up craving for the old days. However, we assume the weakness is in the prescriptions for happiness not in the way our rational brain functions. We tried out new resolutions and followed the latest trends, unfortunately they end up in the recycle bin of our brains within a short time. Nevertheless, we don't ever give up; we do the same thing over and over, expecting different results.

At this point, we must stand firm and decide, choose between Louis and Mazarin.

Though, both Louis and Mazarin are important but much of our energy should be directed towards the Mazarin namely primitive brain without compromising Louis - the rational abilities. In this book I attempt to develop a deep understanding as to how the primitive parts of our brain functions and how happiness come into play. I think such a deep understanding would evoke behavioral changes which would not only help to eliminate our regrets but also would open the door to happiness that lasts.

PART TWO

Can I change?

Revolutionary Advances in Neuroscience

Crucially, it isn't what actually happens to us that makes us unhappy, but how we react to what happens to us. For example, some people become depressed for days after someone laughs at their tie. While others couldn't care less. This raises some fundamental questions about happiness: Why can't we ditch the habits that form the root cause of our unhappiness? Why do we repeat the same mistakes time and again?

This chapter explains the neurochemical basis of our habits. Not to excuse our lack of resilience on occasion, but to help us understand how to bring about meaningful change.

The neurologists were going ape. They had at last reached the final stage of a research project spanning years. In their possession, the brain MRIs of 79 people, taken over a period of four years. From this sample, 39 people, managed to get their cab driver's license after memorising the labyrinthine twists and turns of twentyfive thousand London streets in addition to twenty thousand critical points. The researchers aimed to find out whether absorbing this type of information had caused a change in the respondents' brains. If this could be established it would demolish the longheld belief that the development of the human brain ends at adolescence and could open a new era in neuroscience.

The results indicated that, in people who passed the test, there was a significant growth in the hippocampus region of the brain. The physical structure of the brain had changed during the learning process. Within the control group, no differentiation was observed.[1] Subsequent research[2] has revealed that this change was not only limited to the hippocampus. For instance, it was observed that there have been some changes in different regions of the brain when people gave up smoking, alcohol, overeating or compulsive shopping. People's brains had changed as a result of learning things and changed habits, but most importantly, this continued after adolescence.

This important finding shattered the generally accepted scientific view that it is not possible to change habits and form new ones in later stages of life. We now know that we can change, and that this is possible at any age.

1.

Scenario One: Imagine a bad day. You wake up feeling like you've lost a hundred dollars and found a quarter. You feel upset over the shouting match you had with your business partner (you seem to remember it was a draw) and didn't sleep well because if it. You can't make sense of how you argue about the same things over and over, despite having been in partnership for twenty years. You don't want to be late, so you shave in a hurry and start breakfast. Your daughter approaches you for help with two geometry problems and a bunch of quadratic equations she can't solve but changes her mind when she sees you're tenser than an overwound clock. Your wife asks your opinion about the Knäckebröd she baked. You realize that you might as well have been chewing the lid of a cornflakes box since you're totally unaware of what you are chewing. Your mind is so busy that you tell your wife 'I cannot switch to gourmet mode this early in the morning.' This icy response earns you the Peruvian death stare, familiar to all married men the world over. Despite several apologies she continues to pretend you're not in the building. Killer traffic has quadrupled your stress levels. 'This city it totally out of joint,' you think to yourself. A car swerves in front you without signalling. You slam your fist on the horn. He responds in kind.. Fortunately, the traffic jam breaks up and you reach the office to discover that no one has arrived yet. It seems your workforce's sense of responsibility has evaporated and you are seized with the urge to instigate a mass firing of asses. Then the day starts and you don't talk to your partner until lunch time. A client comes to visit but it isn't a social call. He complains about your service and says he will stop working with your company if you don't take the necessary measures. All afternoon you are busy with what needs to be done to keep this client. In the evening, you drive home through the traffic with a whole barrel load of brand new problems.

Scenario Two: You wake up in the morning. Although you are upset about the quarrel you had with your partner, you know you'll patch things up over a cappuccino at break time. You take a leisurely shower and shave. You enjoy the bread your wife has baked, chat with your daughter about her school and help her with geometry after breakfast. The traffic is congested as usual but you take this as an opportunity to practice your Russian. You enter the office in a good mood and find everybody at work. Your partner is giving you the cold shoulder but you don't really care because you know he'll stop huffing by noon. You meet a client over lunch and listen to his complaints. Then, you delegate this matter to the client's account manager. You don't want to lose this client but you know that even if you do, it won't mark the collapse of western civilisation. You reserve a good table for dinner at your favorite restaurant, buy flowers for your wife and go back home happy as a dog with two tails.

Despite the fact that all of the incidents in these two scenarios are exactly the same, the reactions in the first scenario would result in stress levels high enough to cause cardiac arrest in a buffalo, whereas in the second scenario, happy chemicals are triggered no matter what the circumstances. Hence, it is not the incidents that we need to change but rather our own reactions and habits. This is how we can create a happier world for ourselves.

But, as the man said, 'talk is cheap.' How exactly can we actually do to bring about such a transformation? Before answering this question, let's observe, from the joy.ology perspective, how our brain functions, and how new habits form[3].

2.

We carry around with us, day in and day out, the biggest mystery of the universe. It's situated right between our ears. It looks spongy and feels like jelly. No, it's not a trifle, it your brain. This organ weighs around 1,400 grams. It manages the operation of your entire body using 100 billion processors, called neurons (they're all called 'neuron' which must be confusing when they talk to one another). Each neuron, which operates in a wet chemical-electrical network, has approximately ten thousand connections with neighbouring neurons. Don't stop being amazed, because I'm not done yet. In addition, neurons can send an average of one hundred signals to other neurons — per second! Despite this bind-bogglingly unbelievable complexity, they function almost perfect.[4]

The way our brain works resembles the operation of a company in many ways. For example, in companies, the process of issuing invoices, preparing payrolls and salary payments are routine jobs undertaken by specific people based on standard operating procedures. Therefore, these processes are well known and do not vary significantly each time they occur. Likewise, bodily functions such as respiration, digestion and circulation are automatically managed by specific neuron groups in our brains, just like walking, eating and driving on an empty road. These activities do not require planning or thought.

On the other hand, company functions such as new product development or resolving customer complaints must be handled by teams in different departments. Team structure might be problematic, since it takes a while before team members get used to working together. Initially, communication problems occur between people and coordination becomes an issue as the magnitude of work and the number of people increase. That's why project groups have difficulty in producing efficient results in the early stages of their formation.

Similarly, our brain puts into action different groups of neurons when it rummages through it's extensive filing system for what to do in a new situation, and comes up blank. We experience this when we search for an answer to an unexpected question (Would the speed of light been any different if Einstein's famous equation had turned out to be E=Mc cubed instead of squared?), when we fill in tax forms or learn how to drive. Neurons start working together by chatting to each other over neural networks.

As with project groups within companies, serious adaptation problems occur initially in the brain. Neurons get a bit tongue twisted when they can't initially come up with the right solutions. This is the reason why our thoughts slow down and we produce fewer results when we first attempt something[5] — nobody ever race up a hole in one the first time they hit a golf ball. Stopping the car frequently at gear changes while we are learning how to drive is an example of this. Or we may have difficulty calculating the distance between the car and the pavement while parking. Then, as the job at hand gets harder, the brain mounts an enlistment drive to increase the number of neurons involved in the process, and this brings about even further challenges to coordination and communication. This is what happens when we serve a tennis ball, or tee off in a game of golf.

Interactions between members of project teams within companies strengthen over time and they start performing far better than they did in the initial stages; thus, their output improves in terms of quality and timing.

Similarly, with every attempt, the communication channels between the neurons in the brain expand and the connections strengthen. This explains why repetition is the one and only way to learn something new and achieve perfection at it.[6] If we continue with the golf example, after each and every training session, the harmony between the neurons improve, and over time, our strokes, body position, the way we hold the club and the club angle become things we do without thinking. With every new try, our thinking process gets faster, and our hit rates improve.

But then, what about performance? The corporate performance of a company depends largely on how employees interact and the synergy they create among each other, rather than just the number of employees. Similarly, our mental performance relies on how well neurons are linked with each other, rather than just the number of neurons. For example, it is known that, although the brain of Albert Einstein was 1,230 grams (well below average), the connections between the different parts of his brain were quite well developed.[7]

Furthermore, just as a company seeks to do the job with the least possible number of employees in the shortest time, so our brain strives to function with the least number of neurons via the shortest connections.[8] Both systems are designed to be effective and efficient.

To sum up, imagine an ultra-large company with approximately 100 billion employees. In this company, each employee can give and receive information through approximately ten thousand channels at an average of one hundred messages per second. In other words, an employee can take part in one hundred separate projects per second, thanks to these communication channels. As a result, the company can deliver tailor made solutions to millions of problems that it comes across every single second. And despite these complexities, all processes function perfectly. This is what we do, this is how we are doing and this is who we are.

3.

Everything we have discussed so far should have given you an understanding of the structure and functioning of our brain and of what a jolly useful bunch of fellows our neurons are. Now we can answer questions regarding habits from the perspective of joy.ology.

What is a habit?

A habit is simply a unique reaction to certain effect, stemming from the interaction between specific neurons within our brain. Our brain functions just like an office in which certain responsibilities are assigned to certain people in the event of, for example, a computer malfunction, an air-conditioning failure or electrical problems. Neurons in different regions of our brain are activated for different emotions and behaviors.

How did our habits form?

We are all born with the ability to perceive what is around us, to direct our attention, distinguish between tastes and be scared of bears, wolves, sabretooth lions and the likes. We did not have to develop a connection between neurons to govern these kinds of behaviors. If we'd had to hang around waiting for the right neurons to connect when attacked by a shark, we'd never have gotten out of the swamp. But most of our habits were formed through time. For instance, how much we eat, when to talk, which situations to get angry at are all conscious decisions to a certain extent. The link between the relevant neurons has strengthened by repeating the same conscious decisions over and over. Thereafter, we stopped thinking consciously about these behaviors and they became automatic. They turned into habits. This is how we started carrying out most of our daily activities without a conscious effort.

Why do we find it difficult to change our habits?

Changing habits is somewhat like changing work flows in a company, which can cause overly change-averse employees to sulk, hide under their desks or lock themselves in a toilet cubicle and cry, because it requires forming new project groups for which new definitions and procedures must be established. Yet, people don't want new procedures; they just want to go on doing things the way they always have. That's why Mr. Jones in accounts is still using a manual typewriter when everyone around him is using a MacBook Air.

Similarly, for our habits to change it is necessary for other neurons in our brain to be activated and new communication channels to be established. However, the primitive region of our brain is a stubborn cuss. It really doesn't want to form new channels, so it tries to cling to the existing channels; This is actually why changing habits is so difficult.

How can we overcome this challenge and form new habits?

Charles Duhigg answers this question in his book The Power of Habit[9], through the real-life story of Lisa Allen:

The scientists going through the files of several people since early morning, were exhausted. Still, they were curious as they were going to have the chance to listen to their stories firsthand. For three years, a working group of high powered eggheads: neurologists, psychologists, geneticists and sociologists, had meticulously studied people who managed to give up their addiction to smoking, alcoholism, chronic overeating and shopping. They studied DNA sequencing and medical records, tracked participants' daily routines via in-house cameras and monitored their brains with advanced imaging techniques to measure their reactions to old and new habits.

After a short while, the first participant arrived. The scientists were astonished to see a slim, vigorous, and very attractive young woman. She had no resemblance whatsoever to the overweight woman in the pictures who had pimples, and dark circles under her eyes.

'Welcome Ms Allen. You really look much better than we expected,' said the doctor. 'Will you please share your story with us?' Lisa was very pleased with this compliment and the surprised looks. 'Sure,' she said. 'It all started in Cairo.' Lisa related details of her Cairo trip, undertaken after she discovered her husband had been fooling around with someone else. It was a long time before she could accept

49

her husband's decision to divorce her — he had fallen in love with this other person. The initial stage was grieving, but she then began stalking her ex-husband and his girlfriend, a move not guaranteed to bring about an amicable post marriage calm, I suspect. Lisa followed them, phoned them and one day, perhaps irritated she'd chipped her nail varnish, she threatened to burn down the girl's condo.

Lisa was 34 years old when all this happened. She was smoking, and drinking alcohol and had been since she was 16. In addition, her struggle with obesity continued. This situation with her husband destroyed her already problematic life. 'Things were not on the right track' Lisa said. 'I had always wanted to see the pyramids, and my credit cards were not yet over the limit, so I just decided to go on the trip.' On her first morning in Cairo, Lisa woke early to the sound of morning prayers. She was feeling terrible. She had wept all night, eaten her way through two-thirds of the Cairo Macdonald's menu and now was feeling horribly nauseous. Later that morning, while going through the worn-out streets of Cairo in a cab, Lisa noticed a poor woman digging into garbage. Kids with bare feet kids were playing joyfully. They didn't seem to care at all about their poverty. Lisa then thought of her life, how she did nothing but constantly pity herself. 'I've got to have a goal,' she murmured, 'just like these people. I've got to have a goal.' At that moment, she decided to go on a desert safari. She knew how crazy this idea was; she was so out of shape and with her excessive weight she found it difficult to climb even a few steps. Moreover, she was penniless. She decided to give herself a year to do this. She quit smoking and went on a diet. She started walking, increasing her pace day by day. At the end of the year, she was running marathons. She started a good job and got engaged. Having set her life in order, she had more time for friends. She managed to do all of this in just one year. On the 12th month she went back to Egypt for her safari. Goal achieved!

The researchers, studying Lisa's brain images, observed an extraordinary harmony with her story. The connections between the neurons which govern impulses like eating and alcohol consumption had weakened, while new neural activities had developed in other regions of the brain. With Lisa's persistence, the neurons in charge of habit formation had restructured, strengthening their connections. In short, as Lisa's habits changed, so did her brain.

4.

Lisa was not born into a wealthy family. She had endured serious problems in her childhood and adolescence, and had picked up bad habits due to the influence of friends. And she wasn't lucky with her marriage either, having married a man who would later cheat on her.

Lisa could have held her family and her circumstances responsible for what had happened and allowed herself to become a victim. You will have heard this line before, many times. 'If it hadn't been for my mother, I could have been the prima ballerina with the Bolshoi Ballet!'. Instead, she took responsibility and reinvented herself. She quit her dopamine habits of cigarette smoking and overeating, filling the void this left, with endorphins triggered by her new habit of exercising. In other words, instead of just try to quit her old undesirable habits, she exchanged them for new habits. She also improved her social life and became a more giving and helpful person. She participated in this research to contribute to science and provide help for people who needed it.

Lisa's story and the recent research show us that;

• We are born with pre-established connections between the neurons in our brains, in part so we can run away from that angry hippo that wants to chase us along the river bank without having to think how to do that from scratch.

• New neurons and new connections form under the influence of our experiences and surroundings.

• Our habits and character, in short, who we are, are shaped by these formations.

• For us to change our habits, the existing connections between the relevant neurons must be weakened, while new connections must be developed to replace them.

5.

A simple comparison between the brain and a garden can reflect all the research findings. Soil is essential. Some soil is so rich that anything can grow in it. Throw an apple core onto such soil and come fall you have an orchard. Other types of soil may prove almost barren.

How well you plant, look after and nourish your garden in the early stages is of immense importance.

Well-cared for, your garden will flourish into something akin to the Hanging Gardens of Babylon or the Garden of Eden, perhaps. But, if neglected, you will end up with weeds up to your chin. In this situation, people usually respond with one of three statements:

• 'The soil in my garden is poor, what can I do?' Actually, this is not totally wrong, some people are born much smarter and more amenable, they learn faster and get angry less. Their soil is relatively fertile.

• 'Mom and dad, there's your culprits right there!' We can blame the people who brought us up, the ones who did the first planting and harvesting, so to speak, for not caring enough, not teaching us right from wrong, and allowing our bad habits to develop. There is some truth in this defence too. Yet this approach can lead to inaction and fatalism.

• 'I'll decide how this garden grows from now on!' We can choose to take responsibility for our own life, clean our own garden and plant fabulous flowers. Now, we know this is possible.

Yet, for good results, we need to understand how things roll in the garden, that is to say, we need to understand how our brain works, otherwise, we might actually cause harm, just like an incompetent gardener can damage a garden — by, for example, adding salt to a flower bed instead of fertiliser — and end up making things worse.

To this end, in the next chapters we will study in depth what is going on in our skulls, how happiness and unhappiness form. Let me warn you though – what you are about to read may entirely change your assumptions about happiness! You might be seriously disappointed and feel the need to make some radical changes.

PART THREE

I can't be happy

Cortisol: Destructive Results of Anxiety

Think about this: During your annual performance review, your boss praises you for your efforts, communication skills and achievements. He follows this with a criticism of the way you dress. Of all the things he said, which would most stick in your mind? If you're like me, you'll get hung up on the negatives. Why do we behave this way? Why do positive experiences desert us so quickly, yet negative ones hang around like unwanted relatives after a party? The explanation is as straightforward as it is fascinating. Our brains evolved a negativity bias which helped us survive. Certain receptors in the brain evolved to act like emotional Velcro for bad experiences and Teflon for good ones.

This chapter will help you develop a greater awareness of negativity bias, the unhelpful evolutionary hangover.

It is the year 6,000 BC. Conditions are extremely harsh, incomparable to our world today. There is an unbelievable temperature gap between day and night, never-ending rains, freezing cold and it is very hard to find food. Just for a moment, imagine yourself in this setting. You live daily; you consume what you find on the very same day. Failing to hunt for a couple of days in a row could bring about your demise. Nowhere is safe except for the caves, and you hunt in small groups. An attack by a wild animal is possible at any given moment. A twitch of a tree branch or a slight shadow might indicate approaching danger. You might just become food for a wild animal while you are searching for some.

It is just another day of hunting in the woods, it is very cold, and you have been trying for days now. You are worn out with hunger and have no energy whatsoever to take even another step. Then, suddenly you hear a rustle and you are alarmed. Your whole body is gripped with fear, and it feels like time has stopped – it is difficult to even breathe.

The moment you freeze with fear is actually when an intensive activity speeds up your metabolism. In milliseconds, your brain gathers energy at such a level that might set off explosions in your body, and this prepares you for a reaction which is known as "fight or flight response".[1]

Then, out of the bushes a sabretooth lion appears with a giant roar. You find yourself at the top of a tree and you have no clue how you managed to climb so fast, in spite of all the fear and fatigue. You notice that your fellow tribesmen have also climbed other trees and saved themselves. The tiger is waiting below, prowling fiercely. Then, you and all the tribesmen point your spears at the tiger, and the hunter now becomes the hunted. You eat your fill and have one more day to live.[2]

1.

How can the body reach such high levels of energy? How are we able to run at such a pace or climb such heights that, under normal circumstances, would be impossible for us? Or, how can a tiny woman lift a car to save her child?

I will try to give simple answers to all these questions by comparing the human brain to a warship. This sounds a bit irrelevant, right? Actually, it is not.

Our metabolism reacts to dangerous situations just like an "emergency alarm" on a warship. Just as a frigate siren sounds an alarm if it is at risk of sinking, so our brain raises an alarm if we are faced with a life-threatening event.[3]

On a warship, everything is monitored via sensors which are especially sensitive to sudden changes. If an unexpected deviation occurs, the sensors will set off the alarm system. And in the human brain, the region called the hippocampus functions like a sensor. The hippocampus[4] compares all incidents and events to prerecorded values in the brain. When it detects a significant deviation or a sign of danger, the alarm center of the brain, amygdala,[5] is triggered.

On a warship, alarm settings are preprogrammed. For instance, an increase in pressure, a sudden change in temperature or a rise in the carbon dioxide level will automatically trigger the alarm. These emergency situations were defined based on bitter experience. So, the shipbuilding companies study every accident in detail and specify incidents that are described as "emergency". In many cases, it's not the incident itself, but the likely developments beforehand that are important. For example, at what temperature is there a risk of an explosion? Or, what level of smoke poses a threat of fire? These indications provide warnings in advance to enable the captain to decide upon the appropriate measures.

In our brains, just as on a warship, emergency cases are prerecorded by genetics and bitter experiences.[6] The sound of an explosion, something suddenly hurling at us, or a nearby outcry can set off our internal alarm. We continuously update our definitions of "emergency" based on our painful and upsetting experiences. The hippocampus in our brain automatically records all the developments before the pain is inflicted and later on it assumes that all similar conditions are signs of approaching trouble. This way, we know what to refrain from and we don't have to analyze the potential threats in detail. We can react in milliseconds, and prepare our bodies to deal with approaching threats.[7]

The alarms systems on a warship are designed to take into consideration all kinds of possibilities.[8] However, over time, accidents and extraordinary incidents highlight the need to update the alarm settings in order to prevent a re-occurrence of these unfavorable situations. Since the updates are organized centrally, the alarm systems in all of the warships function in a similar manner.

The basic problem with our brains is that the factory settings were designed thousands of years ago. Therefore, as time passes, mankind has to engage in constant updating. To complicate matters, these updates are made in the light of individual experiences, independently. Due to the lack of a central intervention, human alarm systems work differently, which explains the varying reactions to similar incidents. For instance, back in primary school, a girl in the next class was so afraid of dogs that she would scream at the top of her voice on hearing even the most innocent bark. She became the laughing stock of the entire school and some kids would even bring puppies to class just to terrify her. She couldn't hide her terror even though she knew no real harm would come from these cute puppies. Apparently, she was attacked by dogs when she was a small child and this terrifying experience caused her to be extremely fearful of dogs. In reality, the girl was the victim of an incorrect update to her alarm system. Therefore, it is clear that we need to make the right kind of updates to our alarm systems in order to lead a full and satisfying life or at least to avoid being unhappy.

The alarm in a warship produces an earsplitting sound followed by the rush of crew members. Everyone, including sailors, doctors and even kitchen staff on the ship stop their normal routine and take their position in the staging area. This way, all the crew gather quickly to solve the urgent problem at hand. The maintenance of armory, work in the kitchen and dealing with medical issues are certainly important but there is obviously no point in arranging the seats on the deck or scrubbing a rusty floor if the ship is facing the risk of sinking. All activities are put on hold until the emergency is resolved.

Our internal alarm system does not warn us loudly, instead, it triggers the release of a hormone into the blood which is called cortisol. Cortisol functions like an alarm system in our blood. It prepares us for emergency situations by activating our metabolism.[9] Just like the suspension of routine activities on a warship in an emergency, our brain suppresses functions like growing, reproduction, digestion and immunity until the problem is solved. This is how the saved energy is utilized for solving the current situation and additional energy sources are activated. Our brain causes adrenaline and glucose to be pumped into the blood. It also increases our heartbeat in order to dispatch energy to the farthermost cells and raises the blood pressure by contracting the veins. Also, the amount of cholesterol is scaled up in order to thicken the blood for easier clotting in case of an injury.[10]

The suppression of our digestive, reproduction and immune systems in cases of emergency makes a lot of sense for survival purposes. Just as deactivation of the immune system for five to ten minutes wouldn't bring about hegemony of the microbes, there would be enough time for both digestion and reproduction systems to recover after the danger clears.

On a warship, a yellow or red alarm is triggered depending on the type of the threat. And in our bodies, a low amount of cortisol release causes anxiety, whereas, high amounts lead to fear.[11] On a ship, the reaction to each alarm is different. A yellow alarm describes a preparatory mode and only certain crew members go to the staging area, whereas with a red alarm all activity comes to a halt. The human brain suppresses some functions in case of anxiety, but in the face of fear, all the activities cease except those that are vital for survival.

The alarm indicates that something is wrong, such as abnormal levels of pressure or temperature but provides no information about the source of the problem. It is the captain's responsibility to understand the cause, decide what to do next and assign crew members accordingly. While the technical team looks into the matter, the rest of the crew waits in the staging area for the captain's orders. The captain, thanks to the alarm system, is in a position to take action to resolve all kinds of potential threats to the ship.

The primitive brain gets the message across that something is wrong by increasing the level of cortisol in the bloodstream. It stores the amount of explosive energy necessary for either fighting or escaping. However, it is the rational brain's job to find the reason for the threat and then determine the next steps. The primitive brain maintains the preparatory mode of the body while the rational brain evaluates the options.

The technical team assesses the source of the problem in a short time, and the captain then gives the orders as to what to do. When the danger has been overcome, all crew members return to their normal positions and resume their routine tasks.

Similarly, the rational brain is quick to define the threat and determine the best course of action. For example, in the case of a potential fight with a person bigger than we are, we choose between the option of using force or running away. Once the threat is over, the heartbeat slows down, the blood pressure and the amount of glucose in the blood returns to normal levels and the suppressed body functions, such as the immune, digestion and reproduction systems resume their routine activities.[12]

2.

In summary, we can consider the "fight or flight" reaction as a process consisting of two phases:

Phase 1: Alarm and preparation

Phase 2: Energy explosion

In the preparatory phase, upon detecting danger, the body gathers the energy necessary for a "fight or flight" reaction. Then, it deploys this energy either to escape from the danger or fight it. The process is designed for the momentary solution of an emergency.

Why emergency and why momentary? This is because, during the Paleolithic age, mankind had to produce solutions in minutes or in

just seconds. We were either hunted by the sabretooth lion or managed to run away. But, whatever the outcome, these incidents did not
last more than a few minutes. Therefore, our reactions to dangers are
designed for problems that have solutions which take minutes or even
seconds.

3.

It is 2017. You arrive at your office in the morning. You are late for
work because you couldn't wake up on time. You quietly go to your
desk just hoping that nobody notices you're late. Something is different; you can definitely sense a kind of tension in the air. At first, you
start working as if nothing is wrong and try to observe what is going
on around you. Then, you decide to ask your manager's assistant if
something has happened. She looks at you with astonishment and asks
"Haven't you heard? It's been announced that we're being bought out
by a global company called Talente." You are overwhelmed with initial shock, and just then your manager comes out of his office, quite
angry and approaches you and asks why you are so late. He accuses
you of being irresponsible and lacking concentration. The whole
speech is delivered at a volume that all your colleagues can hear.

Your heartbeat accelerates, all muscles strain and your blood
pressure reaches a level that almost ruptures your veins. You can feel
the accumulated energy in your body. At that very moment, an inner
voice tells you to strike back and put your boss in his place. However,
you are aware of the severe consequences this response could have on
your career, so you remain silent. All the accumulated energy just ex-
plodes within you.

Your boss leaves the office, everybody who witnessed this incident
goes back to work but you remain incensed, your whole body is shaking with anger. You think about how unfairly you were treated. Then,
suddenly you recall the acquisition scenario and that there will almost
certainly be layoffs. You have a mortgage, your daughter's tuition
fees and other loans. With these commitments, you feel terrified at the
thought of being unemployed. You start calculating how this incident
with your boss might influence your position in the company. Your
internal alarm won't stop. You feel the knots tighten in your stomach.

4.

Now imagine yourself as a crew member on a warship, and there are several alarms on your ship every day. With each alarm you rush to the staging area, wait there for a while and then go back to your work. The alarm goes off over and over, just as you are focusing on your work, causing you to not only lose a lot of time but also, responding to alarms is exhausting. How long will you be able to keep this up?

Or alternatively, consider this scenario. The alarm rings and you run to the staging area and wait, however, this time you wait for hours, and then days pass before the captain is able to make a decision or produce a solution. The alarm keeps ringing and you wait with the rest of the crew. Meanwhile, the weapons are unattended, the kitchen is not in operation and there is no maintenance activity in progress.

This all may sound quite absurd. However, this is exactly the kind of life that modern man leads today and is the reason why we can't find peace of mind. Now, think of the number of times you get angry during a day, and consider that your internal alarm activates every time. The traffic, air pollution, financial problems, fears of unemployment, problems at work, desire for status, jealousies. Dealing with these can be exhausting and consumes the time that could alternatively be used to improve our quality of life.

Secondly, there are periods when our internal alarm goes off and is not easily stopped. If we go back to the example of the company takeover, even rumors would be enough to activate your alarm, because similar acquisitions in the past have resulted in extensive layoffs, creating very difficult times for many people. The primitive brain deals with such bad news with its only available response, which is to prepare for the "fight or flight" response. To this end, while the brain pumps energy into your veins, it also suppresses several bodily functions including those that consume energy, such as the immune system.

I can guess what you are thinking now. You find it illogical that your body stores physical energy to deal with an unknown even with an unknown timing. But don't forget – the primitive brain doesn't question. It just moves forward using the factory settings. As a result, unless they are updated, these settings cause a repeat of the same reactions as they did in primitive ages.

Meanwhile, the rational brain tries to comprehend the developments and find a way out. Except that the problems we face in modern times are quite different to those faced by our early ancestors, and far more complex. For example, it isn't even definite whether the takeover will occur. Even if it does, it is not going to be before the end of the year. Besides, the source of the threat is unknown. If there are to be layoffs, who will be in charge of this? Is it going to be colleagues, human resources, the existing management team or teams from the acquisition company? And what will be the criteria for layoffs? Will it be based on performance, experience or interpersonal skills? Yet, despite all these uncertainties, the primitive brain persists in coming up with a solution. It stays in alarm mode until rational brain finds a way out. As a consequence, we spend most of our time speculating on what is going to happen and produce patterns of behavior to fit these imagined scenarios. We realize this is nonsense, but we can't help it.

In brief, just like the crew who can't continue its routine activities if an alarm has sounded, our body too, can't function properly when cortisol circulates in our veins. Apart from making us unhappy, this actually threatens our health.

5.

The ringing alarm doesn't mean that the ship will sink. Yet, the crew reacts as if it will, because there are two types of mistakes at open sea:

1. For the entire crew to respond to an alarm for an unimportant event.

2. Failure to respond to a crucial event.

If the first type of mistake occurs, once the situation is clarified everybody returns to their positions to resume their work, whereas with the second type, all the crew pays the price with their lives. That is why, for maritime safety, all systems are designed to avoid the second type of mistake at all costs, even if this means making the first mistake hundreds of times.

Cortisol entering our blood doesn't mean that we are going to die. For example, we know that an insult during a meeting is not the end of the world – it's like a bee in the car that won't kill us while we are driving. Nevertheless, after an insult, we act as though we will die if we don't respond. This is because, in ancient times, we were faced with two types of mistakes;

1. To take alarm at the twitch of a tree branch, thinking it was a wild animal approaching.

2. To ignore the twitch of a sabertoothed lion, thinking it was the sound of the wind, or bird etc.

If we make the first type of mistake, our body becomes alarmed and gathers energy for no reason. Everything then returns to normal when the sound is identified, and the accumulated energy is then spent during the day. However, if the second mistake is made, the price is a human life. Because of this, mankind survived and evolved by making the first type of mistake hundreds of times to prevent the second type of mistake. This causes us to be extra sensitive to negative perceptions while hindering positive ones.[13] As an example, let's assume that your boss has praised you for your efforts, communication skills and achievements during your annual performance review, and follows this with a criticism of the way you dress. What would be your thoughts after this meeting? What would you remember of the things he said? Research shows that, while positive feedback loses effect in a short space of time, negative feedback endures for years to come.[14]

As a result, positive feedback just slips away due to insignificance, compared with the survival perspective. We all want to be happy, but we turn a blind eye to words and behaviors that can achieve this. On the other hand, we produce disaster scenarios when we receive a small criticism, just the way our ancestors did when they deemed a twitch of a tree branch to be wild animal.

6.

In a recent experiment, respondents in two separate groups were asked to evaluate a new medical procedure. The first group was told that the procedure is a huge breakthrough in medicine and had a 70% success rate. Similarly, the second group was told about the importance of this medical breakthrough and that the procedure had a failure rate of 30%. The respondents' evaluations were then collected;

the first group were positive about the new procedure, while the second group expressed serious concern, even though both groups were informed about exactly the same procedure.

These results are not surprising because we all know that we act with a positive state of mind when we focus on "gain" and negative when "loss" is what we concentrate on. In many cases, our emotions depend on whether we see the glass as being half empty or half full.

The researchers were actually trying to find an answer to a more essential question, which was, how transitions occur between positive and negative psychological states. For this, they explained the medical procedure to the first group from a negative perspective and to the second group from a positive perspective. After then, the first group's opinion changed to negative, whereas there was no change observed in the second group.[15]

	Group 1	Group 2
Probability	70%Success	30%Fail
Response	👍	👎
Probability	30%Success	70%Fail
Response	👎	👎

Transitions Between Positive and Negative Psychological States

The experiment was repeated for different scenarios; however, the same results were received every time. When we evaluate something that we deem positive from a loss perspective, we easily slide to negative. However, the same effect is not observed when we evaluate the negative from a gain perspective. In other words, we easily switch our psychological state from positive to negative, but once we're in a negative state we tend to get stuck there.

To further clarify, anything good, such as a reward for a successful project or praise from top management, takes us off the ground, but this feeling of bliss doesn't last long. We go back to our normal state in a couple of hours. On the other hand, a negative feedback or even a glance might turn our psychological state upside down, which can persist for days. We just can't expel from our minds what has happened, no matter how hard we try. Well, why do we hold on to the failures and the negatives, and allow happiness to slip so easily from our minds? What is happening inside our brains?

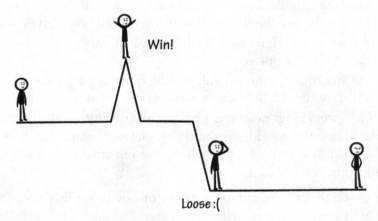

The Win and Loose Perspectives of Mood Change

If we evaluate this from the joy.ology perspective, our brains get alarmed and terminate the flow of happy chemicals when stress chemicals are triggered. We experience an abrupt switch from happiness to unhappiness. Cortisol in our blood prevents our happiness by limiting the effects of dopamine and serotonin.[16] We have a hard time in seeing and feeling the good things in life. Moreover, when cortisol remains in the system too long, it causes excessive activation of the sensitive sensors in the hippocampus region of the brain, and this leads to poor functioning.[17] The hippocampus begins to generate inconsistent signals when it fails to gather healthy information and because of this, the amygdala, the alarm button of the brain, becomes more sensitive.

The system gets alarmed by almost anything. Our reaction in times of stress is out of proportion because the brake system of our brain is cut out. If we go back to the company acquisition example, we start to become oversensitive; the harsh tone of our manager, our colleague's late response to our phone call, and our friends' indifference to what we share on social media might become problems for us. Things that we wouldn't care about otherwise start occupying our minds. We just can't get back the control, even though we know we are being irrational.

In summary, our brain's stress reaction mechanism is designed to protect us from physical threats. For instance, let's say you work as a ranger for a national park, if you are confronted by a bear while out on patrol, your default alarm settings will provide the required energy to fend off the danger. However, if you work in an office environment;

• The stress reactions you produce against various problems during the day will wear out your body

• The stressful condition will last for quite a long time when the source of threat, unlike the bear attack, is undefined.

• The prevailing negative perspective during stress blocks our ability to notice the good things and this fuel our pain, fears and anxiety. We get into a vicious circle where the negative reduces the positive and triggers more of it.

In short, today, the default settings of our brain lead to a bottleneck which hinders the penetration of happiness into our minds. Life keeps on flowing but we just can't be happy.

Well, what about our health?

7.

I must confess that I was not so concerned about the effects of stress before I started working on neuroscience. In fact, I even considered the discussions about this matter to be exaggerations. Yet, having delved deeper into studies related to this subject, I realized that the findings are too significant to be glossed over. In fact, the accumulated knowledge has reached a level where a new field has been established called "psychoneuroendocrinology" which studies the relationship between stress and disease.[18] According to the latest research, stress not only causes diseases such as influenza, diabetes, heart attacks and cancer but also delays recovery from illnesses.[19] This is rather interesting, isn't it? The biggest threat to our health is within us! And we just ignore it or we simply don't make an effort to deal with it. Now, please think of things that annoy you or things that you obsess about during the day. There might be problems worrying you that you can't just get out of your mind. Well, have you ever considered how such a psychological state might influence your health? To tell you the truth, until recently I hadn't.

Now, let's study each and every development in our metabolism, starting from the moment we get stressed. With cortisol entering our bloodstream, in other words, with the activation of the internal alarm, we experience an astonishing increase in physical performance. Instantly, we reach a level of strength that is enough to almost move the world. However, the stress reactions harm the internal functioning of our body, just as every alarm on a warship hinders important activities to some extent.[20] It takes some time for the suppressed functions to reactivate. Moreover, every alarm requires a sudden need for energy, whatever the level may be. To achieve this, our brains rely on our muscles as a source of energy, instead of breaking up the fats in our body, which is a more challenging process. To this end, it transforms our cells from the anabolic mode to the catabolic mode via bypassing of insulin, which is in charge of storing hormones in our body. Thanks to this, we can use the amino acids in our muscles as a direct source of energy. This appears to be a magnificent system to provide instant explosive energy that our body needs. However, when stress becomes chronic,

• Ignoring insulin for a long time causes insulin resistance in our body and paves the way for diabetics.[21]

• Anabolic mode of our cells causes weakened muscles and even muscle breakdown in the longterm.

Moreover, when stress in our body prevails for an extended period of time, a similar situation emerges in our body that is similar to that on a warship, in which all the functions are interrupted due to a state of alarm that lasts for many days. That is because cortisol, which is the alarm siren of our body, is designed to generate instant and short term reactions. When cortisol is released into the blood, our brain suppresses the immune system, along with other body functions in order to save energy. This is why people under chronic stress get sick frequently.[22] For instance, a research on blue collar workers shows that visits to the doctor almost double and the rate of sick leave increases by 50% during periods of stress such as an economic crisis and layoffs. Another research study reveals that people who work in a stressful environment take 30% more sick leave compared with those who do the same job in other companies, but under less stress. In Japan, deaths due to work related stress have reached such high levels that there is now a special term for it: Karoshi.[23]

Despite these startling statistics, you may be thinking that increased sick leave, visits to doctors, and even deaths might be caused by non-stress related factors. Frankly, I wasn't so convinced myself, however, a research study that was carried out among drama students at the University of California clarified these questions in my mind.[24]

The objective of the research was to investigate the effects of stress on the immune system. The students were divided into two groups. The first group was assigned scenarios with fearful elements and the second group with joyful elements. The students were also asked to prepare for their roles by imagining their own, similar memories prior to acting. Students with fearful scenarios in mind would go back to their bitter experiences and the students with joyful elements, to their happy memories. Blood samples of the students were collected after their performance. The results show that there was no change in the immune systems of the students who had joyful scenarios, whereas there was a marked decline in the number of immune cells in students who had stressful scenarios. So, even an unreal situation, based on imagined scenarios, negatively impacted the students' immune systems and increased their vulnerability to infection. This demonstrates that frequently encountered reallife incidents have longterm consequences that could destroy our health.

This is pretty depressing, yet even worse is the fact that it is not only our immune system that is so adversely affected by stress. The special measures that our bodies take in order to gather the explosive energy for the "fight or flight" mode, and then transfer it to the most remote cells are also quite troublesome. For instance, rugged particles, which resemble the texture of sandpaper, form inside our veins due to continuous changes in our heartbeat. Then, when sticky formations in our blood gather around them, these particles turn into scars, which clog the arteries. Heart attacks are the outcome when these scars are in cardiac veins and strokes when they are in the cerebral veins. However, the main problem is the constant straining of the veins during long periods of stress. This is basically a precaution that our brain takes in order to increase the blood pressure, but it leads to a loss of flexibility in the veins, and in turn to arteriosclerosis (the stiffening of the veins).[25]

While all this happens, our brain motivates us to eat more in order to substitute for the energy loss and prepare for potential threats.[26] Our factory settings are designed on the assumption that the dangers will be short-term and that there will be energy shortages afterwards. This is why we lose our appetite during the initial stages of stress but start eating above average later on. Besides, at times of stress, our brains direct us to consume carbohydrates, which are immediately transformed into lipids. This explains our consumption of chocolate or fast food, all high in calories, after upsetting or annoying incidents.

Our brain suppresses digestion for energy saving purposes and reduces the level of mucus production to a minimum level which is in responsible for protecting our stomach. We eat more but digest less. Stomach ache is the immediate outcome but gastritis or even ulcer might be the longterm consequence.[27]

8.

Another weakness of our primitive brain is how it fails to distinguish between reality and fantasy, but reacts similarly to both. This is why even the thought of failure or humiliation is enough to induce the production of stress chemicals which is a prerequisite for the "fight or flight" mode.[28]

Imagine that you are about to speak in public. You approach the stage, and as your name is announced you start thinking that you might make a mistake; at that very moment the audience becomes a threat to you. Your body interprets this as physical danger and immediately starts preparing you for the "fight or flight" mode. However, such a reaction doesn't help but instead creates confusion. The primitive brain searches for ways to deal with the perceived threat and finish the task at hand, while the rational brain tries to focus on the speech. As a result, an experience that might have been pleasant becomes something you want to be over with as soon as possible.

Since pessimistic people are always on alert, it is very difficult for them to be happy.[29] If we go back to the example of the company acquisition in the previous chapter, in such cases, pessimists prepare themselves for the worst possible scenarios. They imagine they will be fired, won't be able to get another job and won't be able to get support. But, they are unaware of the fact that their body is reacting as if already in their disaster scenario and that they are in fact suffering for things that haven't even happened yet and maybe won't ever happen.

Our bodies produce similar reactions when we recall bitter experiences of the past. It switches to alarm mode and doesn't get out of it easily; we worry for absolutely no reason. Moreover, this mental state saps our energy and our ability to develop strategies to improve the quality of our lives. We are hostage to feelings of hatred and hostility, and that is why we can't find happiness unless we forget, forgive and make peace with our past.[30] Cortisol in our blood won't let this happen.

9.

Is a little bit of stress good for us? You might think the release of glucose and adrenaline will boost your performance and thus will make you feel more alive and energetic. Yes, stress can be helpful sometimes but it causes panic and creates deadlocks in most cases. Therefore, instead of getting into an argument about whether or not stress is good, let's try to determine under which conditions it is good and when it makes life more difficult.

Well then, "When is stress good?"

I got a clear answer to this question from Daniel Pink,[31] who perfectly explains a subject through a very simple candle experiment.

Imagine yourself in an empty room. On the table in front of you there is only a candle, a pack of pushpins and a matchbox. Your objective is to make sure the candle stands parallel to the wall when it is lit, but the candle must not touch either the table or the floor. What would be your solution?

Initially, the majority of participants attempt to use the pushpins to attach the candle to the wall, but fail because the pushpins are too short to do this. Then, they try to stick the candle to the wall by warming the edge of it. This doesn't work either. Actually, the solution is to empty the pushpin pack and fix the empty pack to the wall and then place the lit candle in it. It's pretty simple, isn't it? But it takes a while for people to come up with this solution because we don't consider the pushpin pack as being useful. We first try the familiar methods but only when they don't work, then we try to understand the problem by looking at it from different angles. Failing to produce a solution paves the way to creativity, and we discover the pushpin pack after we stumble for a while.

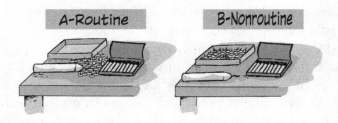

Candle Experiment

Now let's go back to our initial question. Would stress help in such a situation? Would it accelerate the solution?

In order to answer this question, Prof. Dr. Sam Glucksberg of Princeton University decided to run this experiment with two separate groups. With the first group, $150 was offered to the person who solved the problem in the shortest time, and a $40 reward to those in the top quarter. As for the second group, Glucksberg said he just wanted to observe how long it would take for them find a solution. This way, he created a kind of pleasant stress in the first group and the second group was completely free of time constraints.

But then, how did this affect performance?

We would expect that the first group, which was offered a reward, would be faster, however, exactly the opposite occurred. For the first group, the average amount of time to find the solution turned out to be four minutes higher compared with the second group. The same experiment was repeated several times with different participants with the same results. The potential pressure related to the reward was enough to significantly degrade performance, not to mention what would happen if there was a threat of punishment.

Glucksberg then made a small revision to the experiment and started it after he had placed all the pushpins on the table. Now, the participants walked into the room to find a candle, a lot of pushpins, an empty pushpin pack and a matchbox. The experiment is repeated, but now with different results. The first group, which was promised a reward, destroyed the second group.

In summary, stress boosts our performance when the solution to the problem at hand is more obvious to us, but has a negative effect when the solution calls for creativity.

But why is this so? Let's answer this from the joy.ology perspective. Stress forces us to attain results as fast as possible. To this end, the primitive brain comes into play and scans the existing records in its archive. We are able to produce a solution immediately if a record of it exists in our brain, in other words, if it is a familiar incident from the past. However, in case of a situation we are unfamiliar with, stress leads to a dead end because the primitive brain resorts to useless solutions repeatedly, instead of giving an opportunity to the rational brain. As a result, we can't achieve much progress in spite of all our motivation and efforts. We manage to stay much calmer in the face of problems when we aren't under stress. The primitive and the rational brain cooperate and work in perfect harmony when we aren't under pressure. Thanks to this, we can develop alternative perspectives and come up with creative solutions.

Please imagine the things you have to do on a typical day. What kind of candle problems do you face? Are you presented with pushpins in a pack or scattered on a table?

As a result;

• *A small amount of stress might prove to be useful* if you work for a company where no creativity is required and the job descriptions are all set in detail.

• *Stress will lead to a deadlock* if people are expected to generate solutions for different problems every day.

9.

Can we get used to stress? Today, stress is an integral part of people's lives. Some become accustomed and even enjoy stress because of increased adrenaline when confronted by pressure. Therefore, many people don't try to change their current situation, which actually poses a serious threat. However, remaining under intense stress is like staying on Mount Everest after having reached the summit. You may think that you are adapting to the changing conditions as you climb. Actually, camps at different levels of the mountain make adaptation easier. You may think that it is possible to deal with the low pressure and lack of oxygen when you reach the top. Moreover, you think there are people around you and if they can do it, you can too.

This is what happens to us in our modern world. We get used to the traffic, everyday rush and the competitive environment in the workplace. Over time, we come to accept destructive conditions. This acceptance is made easier since many people around us experience the same things. We comprehend the pointlessness of this stress when we leave Mount Everest, get another job or travel abroad. For instance, this is why people are so fascinated when they visit the Scandinavian countries. The well-established system and stress-free life lead us to question our own lifestyle and ask ourselves if it is worth it. However, once we are back at work, we carry on as usual.

In addition, many people believe that they have adjusted to this state of stress and can't even imagine that a better life is possible. However, our physiology is not designed for longterm stress. A stressful environment is deadly destructive, just like living on the summit of Mount Everest, which causes the collapse of multiple organs and damages a number of body functions.

Let's recap. Stress fattens,[32] stupefies,[33] causes depression,[34] makes us sick[35] and delays our recovery,[36] and as a result, we lead an exhausting, unhappy and shorter life.

10.

Charlie Chaplin tells a terrific joke in one of his shows, which makes everybody almost cry with laughter. Chaplin then repeats the same joke, but this time it yields just a few laughs. The third time, not even a single laughter is heard. Charlie Chaplin then asks the audience, "If you don't laugh more than once for the same joke, then why do you cry more than once for the same bad news?" The audience is taken aback by this. Chaplin was correct.

As a matter of fact, we find it rather meaningless to be upset for the same thing continuously and wish we could just stop doing so. But, we fail to get the negative things out of our minds. We know that we are being irrational, yet we can't help it. We fail to influence the primitive region of our brain which governs our emotions. Our factory settings won't allow it. However, if we learn ways to trigger the happy chemicals, we can improve our experiences of happiness, and make a better life for ourselves. In other words, we can upscale the joys even though we can't downscale the sorrows.[37]

Let's see how we can manage this.

PART FOUR

I did it!

Dopamine: Humble Beginnings, Giant Dreams

We feel rewarded by our daily accomplishments: Solving a difficult problem, crossing something off our to-do list or getting intimate with someone. All of these activities give us a buzz. Before congratulating ourselves too much however there's something you need to know. This reward based behavior is intimately connected to the release of remarkably powerful hormone called dopamine, a substance capable of flooding our brains with happiness. A round of applause for dopamine then! Not quite. Gambling, alcohol, cigarettes and drugs can trick your brain into doing something worthy of reward. The feel-good flow of dopamine can occasionally lead to serious addiction and emotional instability. So, I wouldn't offer dopamine a standing ovation just yet.

In this chapter, you will find out how you to develop a sustainable dopamine experience while avoiding dopamine shortcuts that bring only misery in the long run.

It's after 1 P.M. and I'm working on my newly-formed obsession, a giant Mona Lisa puzzle consisting of three thousand pieces. At least two hundred pieces remain in the box. My rational side says, "Go to bed now and you will finish it tomorrow," but I don't feel sleepy at all; every single piece renews my energy. I feel surprisingly fresh and vigorous after five long hours of working on the puzzle, and I know that I won't be able to sleep before I finish.

Now it's your turn! I'd like you to imagine something you wish to accomplish in either the short or long term. It could be completing a project, buying a car, finding your ideal job, getting a promotion, becoming a superstar, or a super hero, marrying the person you love — the list is endless. In your mind, go to that moment of having realized your dream.

For instance, imagine the ultimate pleasure of driving your dream car down route 66. It's likely to resemble how I feel when I work on my Mona Lisa puzzle. Similar sensation, but with different intensity. This feeling is so strong that it catapults you out of your bed in the morning on a trajectory of joy, in pursuit of your goals. You lose a lot of sleep chasing your dreams but ultimately enjoy the pleasure of achievement. You're not the only one. In fact, we all do this. Our needs, objectives, and motivations may differ but, from Einstein to Michael Phelps to Steve Jobs, each of us without exception is influenced by the same hormones. The physiological reward for success remains the same for everybody—whether that success is solving a puzzle, winning a Nobel Prize, or breaking a world record. When we accomplish something, our brain triggers a magical molecule called *dopamine*[1] and we just feel fantastic.

1.

To understand this process a bit better, let's leap aboard our time machine and head back to the Palaeolithic Age (fasten your seatbelt please). On a winter's day, colder than an industrial freezer, people huddle together in the safety of their relatively warm caves. Just thinking about the roll call of dangerous critters lurking outside triggers cortisol which sends the message: 'Maybe this is a day for staying inside, at least until we run out of provsions. The dry, stale food they have been eating for months makes them daydream about a feast after a great hunting trip. Dopamine triggered by the thought of this delicious feast sets them in motion. Anxiety (cortisol) is replaced by hope (dopamine). This is how they gather the courage to leave their caves.

Outside, Old Testament sized cumulonimbus thunderclouds greet them. The weather is colder than they expect. There were no weather forecasters back then but it feels like it's going to snow. Undaunted, they leave their caves determined and confident. Before long, it actually does start snowing and the sudden foglike whiteness makes it hard for them to find their way. Treeshaking roars from some of the largest carnivores that ever strode the planet turns their optimism to mush and fear takes over. All their initial energy, courage, hope and motivation created by dopamine disappears. Some start questioning whether it was wise to leave their caves. 'Told you so,' they say. Shortly, it stops snowing. Hope is renewed as dopamine returns. They start a pursuit which is likely to last days. During this long trek, any sign of potential prey again triggers dopamine and provides the motivation to go on. They see animals in their range of vision when they climb over a hill top and the primitive brain rewards this sudden development with large amounts of dopamine. All these exhausted people are filled with energy as if they had only just started hunting. They speed up and before long, surround their prey.

2.

Let's adapt this scenario to our present-day existence. It's true that some of us are happy to live a life of limited means in small towns and never take too many risks. However, very few of us prefer this. We are often dissatisfied with where we live or what car we drive, and we clamor for more than a humble lifestyle. Dopamine, triggered by dreaming of 'better' makes us act. We leave our homes before the sun comes up in the morning, work harder than one-armed paper hangers until darkness falls and put up with people we dislike with a passion. From time to time our rational brain reminds us that this is far from 'la vida loca'. That what we are doing is meaningless That life is surely to be lived and not endured. Such thoughts are washed overboard in the excitement created by the primitive brain. Thanks to the dopamine, triggered by small successes and bravos, we feel our goal is near, and nothing can stop us reaching it. Before long we are working insanely hard, trying to squeeze 30 hours work into the only 24 we have. When we bother to come up for breath, we're practically living in the office. If we achieve our goal, the flood of dopamine released by the 'I did it' feeling, encourages us to repeat the same pattern of behaviour. So, we continue our quest for our boss's job, a car with even more gadgets built in, or a mansion to replace our perfectly acceptable house. We keep on work at breakneck speed and we'll continue doing so, just so long as the dopamine keeps flowing.

3.

In short, "dopamine" defines the necessary behaviors for the survival and continuation of mankind and sets us in motion. However, its functions are not limited to this. Thanks to dopamine, we can evaluate our options quickly and make healthy prioritizations.[2] How is that possible? To find out, we must all clamber back into our time machine and return to palaeolithic times.

During the Paleolithic Age, hunters spent many hours tracking their prey. In the process, they expended enormous amounts of energy and, as a result, their catch had to provide more calories than they burned hunting for it. Mankind's survival depended upon this simple equation. In the absence of modern calorie-calculating technologies (or a conscious understanding of this premise), dopamine helped to make this distinction between potential prey. Today, not much has changed. We'll still take a night bus across town for a mega-calorie hamburgers with double French fries, because such foods trigger large amounts of dopamine. Food with fewer calories triggers less dopamine, which is why we find it less tasty. This explains why vegetables are not as popular or addictive as bacon cheeseburgers. We even season our salads with high calorie sauces to improve the taste—because we are in constant search for increased dopamine.

Moreover, when a need becomes more critical, from a survival perspective, the primitive brain changes the body's priorities by escalating the dopamine level. For instance, many of us can think of nothing but food when we're hungry, resulting in a loss of focus. Our knowledge of the fact that human beings can survive for 10 days without eating—or that the pizza we ordered will arrive in half an hour— doesn't change this state of mind. That's because the primitive brain sees hunger as a matter of life or death. Therefore, the food we consume when we are very hungry seems more delicious and more satisfying. The same holds true for our goals and accomplishments. Our brain promises us more dopamine (more joy, anyone?) for significant achievements; basically, to keep us on track, ensuring that we pursue goals which contribute most to our survival and to the continuation of our species.

In short, we make our choices today the same way we did thousands of years ago, we favor the options that bring the most happiness. In the modern world, dopamine determines which job or project we will choose—just as it determined which animal to chase in primitive ages. Completing an important project, passing a test, or getting promoted to a better position is more meaningful thanks to dopamine.

4.

Now, look at yourself in the mirror. Carefully. Go through the list of things that make you happy. How many of them contribute to your survival, or to the purpose of continuing mankind? Consuming high-calorie food? Watching a movie? Playing computer games? Smoking or drinking alcohol? Today, the relationship between dopamine and survival has become very complicated because while our primitive brain — custodian of dopamine stocks — is still responding to palaeolithic conditions, our rational brain seeks ways to abuse this situation. And it is quite good at it. We introduced to this concept under the heading of "We deceive our brains". Now let's put that statement under the microscope.

Shortcuts to Dopamine

5.

The first step of this deception was taken approximately five thousand years ago, with the Agricultural Revolution. We managed to grow crops and domesticate wild animals, meaning that humans no longer had to walk for days and hunt to find food. Still, our primitive brain—unaware of this monumental achievement in civilization—went on rewarding high-calorie food consumption with dopamine. Yet, our primitive brains, slow on the uptake, went on rewarding high calorie food with dopamine. Food transcended its basic purpose of survival and featured prominently on the route map to happiness. People started eating not only to satisfy their hunger, but also to feel good. The results have been in many ways catastrophic: A tremendous increase in diseases related to obesity, unbalanced diets and epidemic illnesses.[3] The average life span dropped from 32 years to 20 years and didn't recover to its original level until the nineteenth century, approximately nine thousand years later.[4]

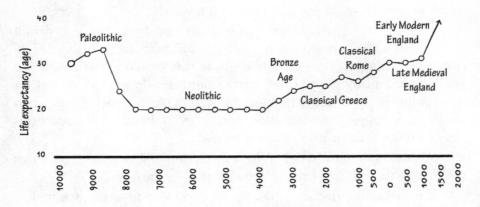

Life Expectancy at Brith by Era

High calorie food remains a huge attraction, we live in the dietary shadow of the chicken nugget. Most concerning of all is that we can't resist even though we know that these foods are the root cause of so many of our contemporary health problems.

Dopamine is also the source of our pleasure when we watch a movie, listen to music, or play a game.[5] Our primitive brain can't distinguish movies from real life situations. Moreover, the mirror neurons in our brain help us identify with the characters, and we perceive movies as personal experiences—as if we were the characters on the screen. That's why movies usually have happy endings—screenwriters want us to have positive feelings at the end of the film.

As for music, we enjoy it because we love guessing a tune.[6] Our primitive brains evaluate every correct guess as an achievement and reward us with small doses of dopamine. That is why we don't take too much pleasure from hearing a song for the first time because we can't take a guess: No guess, no achievement—and therefore, no dopamine. As our ears grow accustomed to the tune, we start making correct guesses and begin to hum along. Dopamine scales up through this learning process and completes its function when we finally memorize the whole tune. This explains why a song declines in popularity after a while; the primitive brain gets bored when guesses become easy. Guesses are no longer significant achievements after memorizing it and — mean spirited character that it is — scrimps on the amount of dopamine it's willing to hand out as a reward.

When it comes to games, the truth is that they create a virtual world which the primitive brain can't distinguish from reality.[7] The primitive brain perceives the situations in this virtual world as real life challenges, and therefore every extra point, new level, and record set in a game is rewarded with dopamine. People feel delighted when they achieve big successes in these games, even though those successes may be unrealistic or unobtainable in real life .

What about gambling? Why can't people stay away from this vice, given the rational brain's knowledge of its dangers?

If we examine decision making phenomenon in detail, we realize that our primitive and rational brains function according to very different principles. They're like next door neighbours that never speak to one another. Our rational brain views the world as an infinite number of possibilities whereas the primitive brain assesses options as black or white, in or out, good or bad.

For instance, we know how unlikely it is to win money on a slot machine. We can even calculate exact numbers like seven percent or thirteen percent as probability rates for various games. However, for the primitive brain the probability is always fiftyfifty. It cannot perform deeper estimations. The dopamine released by the promise of winning thousands of dollars in return for a small stake creates an irresistible desire. Winning infrequently reinforces the faith of the primitive brain. In this manner, short cuts to success are established in our brains and there's a risk that gambling becomes an addiction.[8] Our rational brain, despite all its efforts, fails to influence the irrational brain.

The same holds for our daily decisions. The primitive brain wades in, elbowing detailed probability calculations out the window and promoting rough likelihoods up our decision trees. As a result, we become indifferent to probabilities and our actions are disproportionate, regardless whether we are head of a family, CEO of a company or a prime minister.

Cigarettes,[9] alcohol[10] and some anti-depressants[11] make us feel good by triggering large amounts of dopamine or by preventing its absorption. Basically, the reason why these substances take us away from our troubles and worries is because they directly affect the chemistry of our brains.

But can this virtual happiness substitute for "real" happiness? Studies that employ advanced imaging technologies have revealed that our brain can't distinguish between naturally triggered dopamine and chemically-triggered dopamine.[12] Therefore, there is no difference between real happiness and chemically-created happiness. This is where all the charm resides.

6.

We all want to lead a happier life, and achieving that goal is pretty simple. All we must do is ensure happy chemicals stay in our system for as long as possible. To that end, we have two options:

1. When this quarter's gas bill threatens to hit our letterboxes, we can respond to our primitive brain's call to action by using one or more of the options reviewed above. For example, we might choose to chillax by having a snack or lighting a cigarette. Alternatively, alcohol or anti-depressants can help us shove the gas bill out of mind altogether. A student under pressure can play Grand Theft Auto to get rid of stress. The common problem underlying all these options is clear: They are all unhealthy, unsustainable and they actually detract from finding real solutions to real problems.

2. We can enhance the dopamine experience — get our brains to release more dopamine by realigning our lives to their factory settings. This way, we can lead a healthier, longer, more successful and most important of all, a much happier life. Moreover, these can become the basic principles for happier families and work places. For example, students who score top in university exams see math problems like a game while many others would rather run barefoot over hot coals than multiply one number (pointlessly in their opinion) by another. To them, a math problem is a form of mental torture. Again, highly successful business people say that they take a lot of pleasure from what they do. These people never feel the need to order a crate of shortcuts from Alibaba or Amazon because what they do every day already triggers large amounts of dopamine.

The starting point for sustainable happiness is to improve the dopamine experience and enhance daily processes which lead to dopamine release. But, how?

Dopamine Experience

7.

In recent years, dopamine experience has become an area of interest to various disciplines such as psychology and behavioral economics. Mihaly Csikszentmihalyi's book 'Flow' includes experiments and suggestions for improving the dopamine experience.[13] In their works, Dan Ariely[14] and Nobel Prize Winner Daniel Kahneman[15] (guys who know a thing or two) show how to adapt this approach to business life. Martin E. Seligman,[16] in his book 'Authentic Happiness', explains how we can attain happiness by focusing on our strengths.

When we review these studies, we gather that it is possible to make not only ourselves happy but also the people around us with a few changes in our lifestyles, work environments and relationships. Now, let's see how we can do this.

8.

Which would you prefer? Hitting the lottery jackpot? Or being paralyzed from the waist down? Sounds like a no brainer, right? Here's a related question: Which do you think would bring you happiness? In 1978, researchers at Massachusetts University studied the happiness levels of people who in the previous year won between fifty thousand and one million US dollars in lottery prizes and people who became paralyzed and confined to wheelchairs.[17] People in both groups were asked how much they enjoyed daily activities like chatting with friends, watching TV or having breakfast. The researchers found that lottery winners did not enjoy these activities as much as paralyzed people. The study was repeated by other researchers and similar results produced every time. Winning the lottery had a worse effect than being paralyzed.[18]

Let's continue with a more familiar example. A family friend of mine settled into a nursing home after her husband died. Her older daughter visited frequently and attended to all her needs while the younger was distant and indifferent. In spite of this, the mother overlooked sacrifices made by the older daughter while appreciating every little gesture made by the younger, and immediately shared it with the people around her. The older daughter felt resentful and blamed her mother for being ungrateful. I am sure you have faced similar situations.

What do these examples show us? From a superficial perspective:

• In order to be happy, we need bad things to happen to us.

• In order to make someone happy, we need to be indifferent them.

Wait a minute! That can't be right, can it? Well, it is possible to draw such conclusions, however, happiness is too complicated to be reduced to such a simplistic concept.

Let's recall how dopamine creates happiness. When we achieve something, our brain rewards us with dopamine and we feel happy. The specific amount of dopamine depends on how much the results meet our expectations.

"Expectations" is the key term here.[19] If we evaluate the above examples within this framework, the lottery winners can't achieve happiness because of their increased expectations in everyday life. A hotel room without the promised view or with a dining room setting with a missing dessert spoon, or a five minutes delay in room service is enough to make them crawl under their beds and sulk. On the other hand, paralyzed people are not hung up on details because of their low levels of expectation and thus small things make them happy. Similarly, the older daughter can't please the mother whatever she does since she raised expectations, whereas even a warm smile of the younger one is enough to melt her. In the case of the older daughter, you can blame the mother for being unfair and ungrateful. However, this would be a harsh judgement because the mother's behavior is entirely influenced by the hormones triggered by her primitive brain.

What about children? Is all of this valid for them, too? Studies show that children from wealthier families are less happy than ones from middle income families.[20] Children's expectations rise when families meet all of their desires. This results in reduced amounts of dopamine, creating kids who can't enjoy the daily activities of life.

Statistics show that in Russia, the suicide rate among children from rich families is twenty four times higher than amongst other groups of children. In the US, this rate is sixteen times higher. It seems that, as a family's potential to meet their children's desires increases, the possibility of those children being happy decreases.[21] Many families, unknowingly, condemn their kids to unhappiness.

9.

It seems that, quite literally, our primitive brains are beyond reason. We cannot control these ancient biological constructions. What can we do then, for our own happiness and also for that of the people around us?

We could start by getting our expectations under control for a start. I am not saying that we should lower our goals. I am just trying to point out the importance of celebrating small achievements and living in the moment. As it is not possible to break sales records or to invent something new every day, we need to enjoy simpler pleasures: Finding solutions to daily problems, making a good presentation and even enjoying a good meal. Let's examine this from the neuroscience perspective. The graphic on the left shows the amount of dopamine triggered when we celebrate small achievements. The graphic on the right depicts the dopamine amount if we celebrate after the achievement. Which one is valid for you? Or which do you prefer?

At this point, it is possible to reach two conclusions:

1. Celebrating small successes on the road to our goals triggers more dopamine than having a big celebration afterwards.

2. Dopamine loses effect after achievement since its basic function is to set us in motion. That is why the joy brought by even the biggest achievements quickly fades. It takes only a few days for it to disappear altogether and then everything goes back to normal.

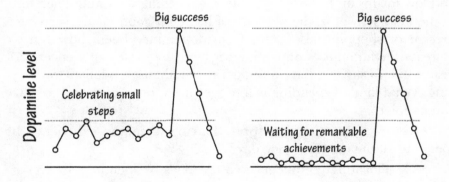

Enhancing Dopamine Experience through Celebration

Therefore, in order to enjoy sustainable happiness, we need to learn how to be happy during the whole experience. In this respect, I find Rick Hanson's approach in his book 'Hardwiring Happiness' rather functional. The approach consists of three steps:[22]

1. Define: Define an achievement you made or a positive experience you had during the day.

2. Enrich: Reflect on this achievement and the experience for a while. Ask yourself questions like, "What is the significance of this success," "What will it provide," and "How will it contribute to my life?"

3. Feel: Feel the joy created by the dopamine which was triggered during the enrichment stage. Internalize this positive experience and don't let it flow away and leave you quickly.

You may find this behavior pattern somewhat odd in the beginning. However, if you engage yourself in it on a routine basis, you will witness how your physiological state will change entirely.

Rule Number 1: Feel your everyday achievements and positive experiences; don't let them flow away quickly.

10.

Dopamine is triggered not only by success but also when we find something we have searched for, like the car keys you've hunted high and low for for an hour.[23] Or achieve something we want. Therefore, in the modern world, the pleasure of having a good meal, receiving a present or shopping also stems from dopamine. Then, how can we increase the amount of dopamine triggered by these experiences? For instance, let's say you have a budget of five thousand dollars for shopping. What kind of spending will trigger more dopamine and so make you happier?

• Going on a shopping spree. Having a unique experience by spending all the money in one day?

• Or allocating the budget to a few days by spending an average of one thousand dollars per day?

Which would you prefer? Approximately eighty per cent of the people who answered this question think that option 'a' would make them happier and this is actually how they live. However, they can't see that they are missing out on huge potential for happiness by preferring this pattern of behavior. The graphic below reflects this; the portion under the dotted line shows the feeling of happiness that remains once the shopping spree is over. Even though dopamine provides us with a high degree of happiness when we reach our desires, this feeling of joy decreases soon after dopamine has done its job. In the graphic above, the portion under the continuous line represents happiness brought by shopping that is done in intervals. In this case, we can't reach a peak of happiness which is provided by rushing into your neighbourhood Apple Store and sweeping whole shelves of gadgets into your bag. yet, our happiness lasts longer. Therefore, it is possible to escalate our happiness by adopting the interval shopping method.[24]

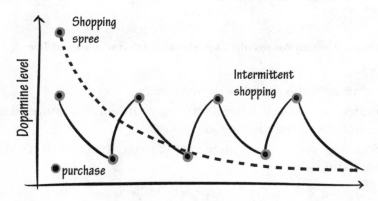

Evaluating a Pleasurable Experience with and without Break

What about boring experiences? And heaven knows there's plenty of those around. Think of activities you dislike. Organizing files in the office, perhaps, or washing the dishes or picking up leaves in the garden. Would you prefer to do these chores at once or finish them in portions? Most people choose to thin slice boring errands into smaller pieces, but is this the right strategy?

In order to answer this question, Leif Nelson and Tom Meyvis carried out research which included two groups. Quite frankly it all sounded a bit nutty, but the results were revealing. In the first group, respondents put on headphones and listened to the sound of a vacuum cleaner at a high volume (see what I mean), uninterrupted for 40 seconds. The second group was exposed to the same noise but at intervals of ten seconds each followed by a break of five seconds. Then, the respondents were asked to evaluate their level of discomfort. The results showed that the second group, the group who had breaks, felt much more uncomfortable compared to the first group. Even though giving breaks had provided short reliefs, the overall discomfort was increased tremendously.[25]

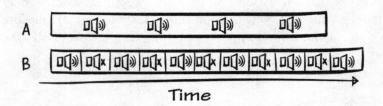

Evaluating an Annoying Experience with and without Break

In summary, these studies showed that;

• Eating a fourcourse meal in twenty minutes is more likely to give you heartburn than lasting joy.

• Breaks given during housecleaning make the work at hand even more frustrating.

Rule Number 2: Divide joyful experiences into parts and, if possible, complete the unpleasant ones without any breaks.

11.

Let's see how we can make our family, friends, employees and customers happy. We need a fundamental change of behavior for this, because we act on the assumption that people will be happy if their expectations are met. Now, we know that this assumption is not a correct one; in the short-term meeting expectations may deliver happiness but in the long term it may lead to dead ends. Despite this, many companies strive to thrash life into clichés like 'The customer is always right' or 'We exist to deliver customer expectations'. They'd be as well trying to thrash life into a dead horse. Does this effort really make customers happy? Absolutely not! Consumer research indicates decreasing levels of customer satisfaction. Complaints persist despite significant improvements in product and service quality. Customers can't be happy because of the uncontrollable rise in expectation, creating a situation harmful to both sides.

Is it any different for employees? A few years ago, I was invited to deliver a speech in a weekend camp held by a company. Managers were preparing breakfast and squeezing orange juice for the employees. At first I was impressed, I have to admit. However, when I talked to the general manager I gathered that all in the garden was less rosy than it seemed.

Top management had been pressed by the board to improve employee satisfaction ratings and many projects were carried out to this end. At first, employees welcomed every improvement with great enthusiasm, but after a while they simply found other things to complain about. The French fries in the cafeteria were the wrong shape, the roller blinds on the office windows too beige, and so on. The management tagged their employees as ingrates and accused them of failing to appreciate what had been done for them. In a few months time, the employees' attitude had started to annoy the board. Improvement initiatives were stopped and many newly assigned rights retracted. Employee morale collapsed like a badly prepared soufflé. The best employees in the company resigned, leading to severe losses. And than, the board decided to change the top management.

Currently, the new management is trying to recover employee satisfaction to its original level again by meeting their expectations — hence repeating the same mistake. In fact, the right course of action should be to learn how to manage expectations rather than to give whatever they want. For instance, in spite of the fact that KFC and Starbucks are among the best employers in the world, they spoil neither their employees nor their customers. Rules are clear. For example, employees can't stretch the rules about breaks whatsoever. They can't demand promotion or a raise in salary.

Let's wrap up. Humankind perpetually strives for more. You can meet a person's every desire but that will only guarantee new demands. After a while, these requests climb to a level which can no longer be satisfied. However, your situation is not understood and you begin to be held responsible for the other person's misery.

Rule Number 3: Don't kill yourself trying to meet the expectations of other people.

12.

If meeting the expectations of other people brings them unhappiness, then what should we do instead? What about cultivating conditions that can make them happy? Let's go step by step.

Once again, imagine you live in ancient times. Conditions are harsh, but life is very simple and basic. You know what awaits you outside of your cave—what dangers and risks you will face, and what rewards will come from your efforts. Now let's come back to the present day. Life has become so complicated that we even find it difficult to answer many of our children's questions, such "Why should I go to school?" or "Why do I have to learn these subjects?" It's not much different in the business world. People feel lost in giant corporations. They can't see what they are a part of, or how their efforts contribute to the end product or service. So, how does the complexity resulting from modernisation, and our failure to see the results of our efforts, influence our happiness?

In order to answer this question, researchers at Kyoto University conducted a study in which they placed participants in two groups. Both groups were given Lego pieces and instructions describing the shapes to construct with those pieces, as well as specific assembly instructions. The first group was told that they would be given twenty dollars upon successful completion of the project, but was not given any further explanation. Twenty dollars was a good amount for an effort of half an hour, but the shapes they were asked to create were incomprehensible. The second group was offered fifteen dollars, and was presented with a picture of a magnificent sports car. The particpants' brains were scanned with an MR device during the experiment, which made it possible to observe their neural activity. Results showed that students in the second group had a higher level of activity in the cerebral cortex[26] of their brains. This indicates that the second group was happier than the first group, even though they were paid less.

According to this example, the better we envisage the activity in our brain the more dopamine our primitive brain releases. In other words, when we can make a prediction about the outcome of an assignment, we have more motivation to complete it and take more pleasure in doing so.

Now imagine the powerful leaders, outstanding commanders, legendary trainers, and inspiring speakers in history. They set people into action by appealing to their emotions. Did you ever think about how they manage to do this? When a powerful leader speaks, he or she describes the future and the steps to achieve it so well that his or her followers experience a high level of dopamine release in their brains. This explains how players on a soccer team who watched four goals sail into their net during the first half of a match can start the second half with a morale boost, as if they're just beginning. Or, how a sales team which failed to sign even one contract during the previous week can start a new one fresh, upbeat, and in high spirits.

In summary, it is possible to raise the motivation and happiness of people by just making the results more visible.

Rule Number 4: Have concrete goals in life.

13.

Let's move on with a familiar story. Three masons are asked "What they do and how they feel". The least happy one goes "Don't you see that I am *aligning bricks*?" The second mason says "I am OK. As you you can see I am *putting up a wall*". The third mason, glowing with joy answers "I am *building a cathedral*".

This story tells us that the meaning we ascribe to what we do is the basic determinant of the pleasure and happiness we get out of it. But, can we prove such a deduction scientifically? This is where joy.ology steps in.

In order to understand the correlation between "created value" and "work motivation" better, let's go through the "Lego Bionicle" (little war robot) experiment which was designed by Dan Ariely[27] of Duke University. Respondents were distributed Bionicle pieces and were asked to assemble them as per the instructions on the box. In return, they were paid on a decreasing scale.

Participants were paid two US dollars for the first robot they built and the amount was decreased by 11 cents for every additional robot they assembled. This is below the minimum wage but this is an experiment so calm down. For the first robot, it was two US dollars, one US dollar and eighty nine cents for the second robot and one dollar seventy eight cents for the third one, and the payment plan went so on. Ariely and his team aimed to find out how much the students were willing to go down in their payments in two separate set ups which they called "work for nothing" and "create value". In "work for nothing" set up, the participants made the assembly by using the same pieces. In other words, the participant handed the robot to the observer upon completion; the observer after checking it disassembled the robot and asked the participant whether he or she wanted to build the same one. In "create value" set up, the observer placed the robot on a shelf instead of disassembling it. The observer gave the participant new pieces for every other robot.

Now, let's see the results of the experiment. The participants in "work for nothing" set up built an average of 7,2 robots. Eighty percent of the respondents in this set up quitted construction when the payment dropped below one US dollar. On the other hand, in the "create value" set up, an average of 10,6 robots were assembled. Sixty five percent of the participants continued working when the payment went down under one US dollar.

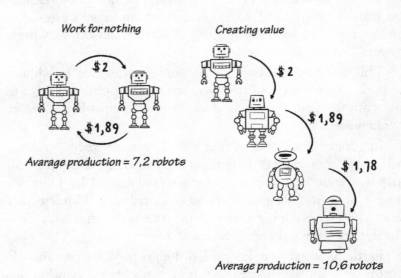

Work for nothing

$ 2

$ 1,89

Avarage production = 7,2 robots

Creating value

$ 2

$ 1,89

$ 1,78

Average production = 10,6 robots

Importance of Meaning

Besides, the participants were asked to evaluate their work after the experiment. The ones in the "work for nothing" set up found the payment insufficient while the participants in the "create value" set up expressed the pleasure they had during the process. Please note that these people were not doing something very important, were just assembling Lego pieces. Seeing the final products on a shelf gave them a pleasure of work and ensured more production with less payment.

In another experiment, respondents were asked to describe their daily activities in detail and their brains were scanned with MR device meanwhile. It was observed that there was an increased activity in the cerebral cortex of the brain which is called the "region of happiness" while they were describing important activities. So, simply imagining activities considered meaningful was in itself enough to make people happy. But, what about the opposite case? How did the brains of people react who believed they work for nothing all day? It was seen that when these people made a review of their day, there was no activity in their cerebral cortex while the amount of cortisol increased significantly afterwards. The results revealed engaging in meaningless activities during the day is a major source of stress.

The Most Cruel Punishment Ever!

Struggling for a few doses of dopamine all day and getting nothing in return...I guess the story of Sisyphus in Greek mythology best reflects the pain inflicted by such a situation.[28] Sisyphus takes the throne from his brother forcefully, murders the visitors and seduces his own niece. On top of that, he gives Zeus away and he deceives Peroshope, the good-hearted queen of the underworld. Now I know that they say there some good in everyone but Sisyphus throws that sociological theory into grave doubt. The gods want to severely punish this greedy and deceptive king and decide that the most severe punishment you could give a man was to engage him in *'useless and hopeless effort'*. Sisyphus was condemned by the gods to push the same rock up a hill. Just as Sisyphus almost reached the top of the hill, the rock would roll all the way back to the bottom again. Sisyphus can't create any value despite working relentlessly every day.

Can these findings be applied in the business world? Research carried out by Talente International in 2012 indicated that forty six percent of blue collar workers think that they produce nothing meaningful. Almost fifty of people are being punished like Sisyphus. We fail to grasp this fact and expect a lift in employee motivation by increasing salaries or modifying the physical conditions of the workplace. The same goes for us. We strive for more income and higher status without questioning what we really do and how we contribute to the good of society. Yet, we tend to forget that none of this alone is sufficient to trigger our happy chemicals. This may be why outwardly successful people starve terribly in their inner worlds. What we really crave is being useful, creating and adding value.

Rule Number 5: Work should be meaningful and add value.

14.

Let's remember our ancestors' basic rule of survival: Calories expended while hunting should be less than calories gained from hunting. Otherwise there's no point. That is why all human mechanisms are based on energy efficiency. That is where our desire to attain more with less effort originates from. This is the reason why so many people dream of winning the lottery or inheriting a fortune. Or why they search for shortcuts to success. But how does this strategy negatively influence our overall happiness?

The ready cake mix, introduced in the late 1940's, was expected to gain a strong position in the market but it didn't. Housewives were reluctant to use these mixes which only required adding some water.

The producers changed the variants and introduced mixes which contained cacao, raisins and cinnamon. Surely these additions would make the bakers' pulses race. But no. This failed too. Ernest Dichter, a psychologist, claimed that these products removed the joy and pride of cake making by oversimplifying the process. After all, the skill of adding water is mastered by most of us at kindergarten — it's hardly on a par with landing the Space Shuttle. So, Pillsbury removed the dried eggs and milk powder from the ingredients. This meant that women themselves had to add fresh milk, eggs and butter to the mix while preparing it. What do you think happened? There was an instant sales boom. This was because the product reached a level of difficulty which a woman with average cooking skills could handle with some effort.

Rolf Dobelli, in his book 'The Art of Thinking Clearly'[29] calls this the 'Ikea effect'. Why? As we know, Ikea sells its products in ready-to-assemble format. After purchase, you have a choice:
• Get professional help to assemble it
• Follow the instructions and assemble it yourself

Research shows that customers who choose to assemble their own furniture feel happier and are fonder of their furniture than people who call in professional help.

In summary, showing effort for something doesn't alter the object itself but influences the way we feel during the process of achieving and afterwards. As the effort increases, the joy brought by success increases too. That is where the dilemma lies. On one hand, our primitive brain encourages us 'to get more with less effort' and on the other, reduces the amount of dopamine when we reach things with less effort since it doesn't view them as achievements. In short, acting inconsistently with our factory settings brings unhappiness.

Rule Number 6: Keep away from shortcuts to success.

15.

The Ikea and ready cake mix cases tell us that we have to make an effort to overcome some obstacles before we can be happy. By contrast, my wife won't even allow such products in the house! And as for

Ikea, I bought a wardrobe from Ikea about five years ago. It fell apart while I was trying to assemble it and I had to throw it away. So, while my wife is disinterested in ready cake mixes because she finds them too easy to make, I keep away from Ikea furniture because I find it too hard to build. This raises an interesting question: To achieve happiness, how difficult must our chosen tasks be?

Mihaly Csikszentmihalyi and his team interviewed more than eight thousand people, from corporate employees to Dominican monks, Himalayan mountaineers to Navajo shepherds. They distributed pagers to these people which beeped ten times a day.[30] And for every time the buzzer went they were asked to describe:

- How they felt
- What kind of difficulty they were confronting at that moment
- To what extent they used their skills against these difficulties?

Respondents were then divided into three categories (Researchers are always dividing people into groups) based on the difficulties they were facing and their skill levels. They found that when the level of difficulty was below their skills, people got BORED. When the level of difficulty was above their skills they became ANXIOUS. In between these two states, there is a critical area which Csikszentmihalyi calls the FLOW. This area is the intersection of the level of difficulty and the full potential of skills. This is where the work provides most pleasure and happiness reaches its peak.

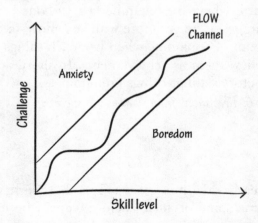

Model of Flow as Related to Challenge and Skill

According to Csikszentmihalyi, at this particular point, people fully concentrate on what they do and don't think of anything else; it is almost like their existence is postponed. They don't feel hunger or fatigue. Even their sense of self disappears.

As I read this, I thought of my nephew. Imagine a boy who sits in front of the computer for hours, who forgets to eat, doesn't feel tired and even confuses what day it is. I am sure this is pretty easy to imagine since many kids today are overwhelmed when it comes computer games (and many parents struggle with what to do when they discover their little angels blowing the undead's heads off playing Zombie Apocalypse VI).

How can these kids commit their full attention and energy to the virtual problems presented by computer games, yet still find it difficult to study for more than half an hour? How could computer games companies create such levels of addiction?

The answer is obvious: By achieving the optimal balance between difficulty and skill. Remember, the initial levels of all computer games are pretty simple. New players are granted the instant joy of success when they first start playing. At first, decapitating a zombie should be as easy as stirring sugar into your tea. Then the game — any good game that is — starts becoming more difficult as players master it and develop their skills. Games are designed around 'levels' which maintain a balance between difficulty and skill, preventing players from leaving the flow area. This way, the player pushes his or her limits in order to deliver the virtual assignment. The joy created by the surge of dopamine triggered by this hard-gained success reaches such a level that it isolates the player from the outer world.

Now, when your child is at such a moment of flow, how do you think he would react if you told him to study an activity that would carry him into the stress zone? You can be certain that his primitive brain wouldn't let him, even though his rational side tells him that he has to study. His mind would still be on the computer game even if he sits down to study. How is it possible, then, that some kids study for hours every day? *The secret is the same: by managing to stay in the flow.* These kids, when they solve a mathematics or physics problem, experience a sensation of success similar to other kids' sense of achievement at computer games. Therefore, kids who manage to stay in the moment of flow become successful whereas others lose their motivation and try to meet their dopamine needs though playing computer games.

As a matter of fact, we experience moments of flow in other learning processes too. In order to master any subject, we need to preserve the moment of flow during the whole process. I recall my first days of learning how to play the guitar. It was really hard to learn the notes and press different strings simultaneously. Yet, I had a feeling that I pulled it off, especially because my teacher's approach made me feel quite talented. I wasn't ever going to be EricClapton but even the squeaks I produced sounded like the best melodies in the world; I travelled to another dimension when I played my guitar. I poured my soul into it and let my talent speak. The notes were flowing and I lost my sense of time. However, as the lessons progressed, I started finding it difficult to play more complicated melodies. I responded by practicing more. Yet, I realized that no matter how much I practiced I couldn't reach the level I desired. This brought me a kind of anxiety and a sense of failure. Moreover, the simple melodies which I mastered no longer gave me pleasure. How did I reach this state?

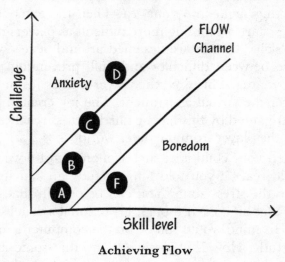

Achieving Flow

Let's look at Csikszentmihalyi's model: Point A in the graphic represents the moment I started learning how to play the guitar. I was working on simple melodies due to my low level of skills and had a high amount of pleasure since I was at the flow moment.

However, my skills were not progressing at the same pace as the melodies, which got harder and harder. Then, I reached the limit of my potential. When I landed at point D, no matter how much I practiced, I couldn't manage to play the new melodies. At this point, I could choose to continue with simple melodies that were in my scope of skills but who wants to play the same tune over and over? Although that certainly won't lead to stress it will take you to point F in a short time where it is dull and offers no joy at all.

Csikszentmihalyi's model provides us with a very simple but powerful framework. Things you accomplish and can can get better at give you great pleasure since they allow you to stay in the moment of flow. Today, a guitarist practices an average of five hours a day, an Olympic athlete eight hours and a qualified academician reads and researches so much, he only comes up for air on average every six hours. If these don't fall within your area of interest, you will find these durations very long and even may feel sorry for these people. Yet, in fact, they feel fantastic as they experience the moment of flow in their practice or studies. This helps them to connect passionately with what they do and brings success and joy as a result.

In summary, our level of happiness varies with the type of challenge we confront and depends on what extent we utilize our potential to overcome this challenge. In our work life as well, we need to maintain a balance between the challenges and our skills in order to achieve internal success and secure large amounts of dopamine in return. Otherwise, huge challenges will result in anxiety and small ones in boredom. Our dissatisfaction will not be resolved no matter how much softer the seats in the staff room get, or salary raise granted. From this perspective, we can say that the challenge/skill balance is the prerequisite for happiness both in our private and professional life.

The Unhappiness Trap

16.

The basic mistake we make is to continually strive to reach the 'BOREDOM' area, even though we feel happiest in the 'FLOW' area. This situation stems from the energy equation previously mentioned. When we have the chance to achieve something easily we immediately drop our efforts, resulting in limited happiness because our primitive brain doesn't recognize or value easy achievements (Again, the primitive brain is the villain of the piece!) No success, no dopamine. The 'boredom' area guarantees you'll feel good for a short time only, however, in the medium or long term it will give rise to a feeling of uselessness or even a sense of void.

This is basically the reason for widespread unhappiness among civil servants. People usually wish to get into the public sector where there is very low risk of losing their job but start complaining after a very short while once they are in. Actually, the underlying factor for their complaints is the never changing salary regardless of how much they work. As a result, they quit their efforts, life becomes routine, their brains stop releasing dopamine and good work conditions don't suffice to make them happy.

People go through a similar experience when they retire. I remember how much my aunt looked forward to retirement. After retirement, she made a world tour and took really long holidays. And now she goes on about how great it is to work and craves the hectic days of her past.

Therefore, to preserve our happiness;

• We need to beware of unhappiness traps and get away the allure of shortcuts

• We need to maintain a sound balance of challenge/skill at work.

Rule Number 7: Stay on the moment of FLOW.

17.

For some, being at work is more pleasing than being at home. That is why they work until late in the evening. All they talk about is work and they won't be detached from it even during holidays. These people who are often described as workaholics are called "dopamine addicts" in joy.ology literature.

For them, work is a unique source of joy. It's why they put work above everything else in their lives; family and friends always come second. Even their relationships are tools for improving their work. When we examine famous artists or inventors from Albert Einstein to Michelangelo or Vincent Van Gogh, we come across evidence of the familiar outcomes of dopamine addiction: huge success, an antisocial personality, a turbulent life with many ups and downs and a depressive state of mind which may even lead to suicide. These extreme examples aside, I have friends who work sixteen hours a day and consume themselves unknowingly.

But then, why do dopamine addicts, for all the joy they get from working, face such negatives in their lives? There are two basic reasons for this:

1. Dopamine addiction causes a vicious circle which is called Hedonistic Treadmill.[31] According to this theory, people who work with success are in fact no different than prisoners who try to go forward on a wheel because;

  a. We feel good the moment we take a step (*Making a progress, achieving something makes us feel good*).

  b. However, as the wheel turns, we find ourselves at our original point (*Feeling of happiness doesn't last long; we go back to our state of mind in a short time*).

  c. We need to take another step in order to feel happy again (*We need new successes to be happy again*).

  d. All this effort takes us nowhere (*Dopamine induced happiness is not long lasting*).

  e. Turning the wheel becomes harder and harder every day (*People long for their youth because the emotions generated by their first job, first car, and first house and there are few to put above these later*).

2. High levels of dopamine addiction cause deactivation of other hormones, starting with oxytocin. We experience this especially when we neglect our family and friends at the expense of success. Through time, our relations are harmed and our ability to trigger other hormones than dopamine weakens. We face two options at this point:

  a. To reinvigorate our relationships, setting aside spare time with family and friends to achieve this.

  b. To devote ourselves to work entirely.

Daily Version of Treadmill

No matter how logical the first option seems, people usually go ahead with the second option and this escalates their dopamine addiction. They end up being a slave to one single hormone. They overwork as they have no other alternatives left to bring them happiness. In short, these seemingly successful people are in reality, pitiful. They enter a painful void when they leave their jobs or retire. It is therefore crucial to point out that there is a thin line between improving the dopamine experience and dopamine addiction.

This tells us;

• Dopamine released at moments of FLOW also brings some risks along with the happiness it creates.

• In order to avoid risks, we need to understand the other happy chemicals and learn how we can improve the experience each can provide us with.

Let's continue with SEROTONINE

PART FIVE

I want respect!

Serotonin: Selfconceit and Arrogance in Charge

Dopamine production is triggered when we accomplish something, making us feel good. When your uncle Barney patted you on the head in third grade because you were a silver medallist in the egg and spoon race, his acknowledgement of your accomplishment caused serotonin - the respect and status hormone - to kick in, making us feel like we just made a trip to the stars and back. We crave such plaudits and admiration just so we can earn another shot of serotonin. Serotonin, however, isn't entirely the best friend we've ever had. It carries risk, just like dopamine. Though the brain is the smartest wetware in the universe (that we know of), it can have its moments. It can, for instance, be tricked by gossip, branding and antidepressants into feelings of false prestige. This can lead to serious addiction and emotional instability, just like dopamine. This chapter will help you identify serotonin traps and explain how we can increase serotonin-based happiness safely.

Well, we know that happiness borne of achievement, is the result of dopamine. When such achievements are appreciated by others, another hormone, namely serotonin is activated and we feel as if we're floating 10 feet off the ground. Admiration escalates our social status, which is why serotonin is also described as the status hormone. Serotonin is the main source of emotions such as feeling more accomplished or feeling superior to others.[1]

The basic difference between serotonin and dopamine is that serotonin requires the praise and acceptance of others. In other words, we are not in control of serotonin activate.[2] Which is a bit of a drag really. This explains why so many people constantly seek the attention and admiration of others, either by their looks or through their behavior. There is not much we can do about this since this is how our primitive brain functions.

The common characteristics of serotonin and dopamine are that both:
• Can be triggered by several shortcuts
• Are highly addictive.[3]

Therefore, as with dopamine, we can deceive our brain into triggering serotonin, and thus attain happiness the easy way. However, doing so could potentially place ourselves in a deeply melancholic and sorrowful state. The best way to overcome this potential risk is to try to understand this hormone.

1.

When he arrived at the airport, the sparrows lay still abed and the waiting lounge was emptier than a spendthrift's wallet. He thought it might be holiday season. The counters were still closed. There was nothing he could do but wait. He approached the seats on his right but changed his mind when he saw a sleeping man draped over a row of seats. How anyone could sleep with an armrest jammed into their kidneys, he did not know. His eyebrows shot skyward when he saw a woman breastfeeding her baby - was that even legal? This scene reminded him of his past, when he was poor. Actually, he wasn't full now, but he planned on having a feast in the CIP lounge, which is why he had left home without having breakfast. Even now, the thought of sitting on those metal seats made him feel uncomfortable.

"Why on earth isn't there a separate entrance for CIPs?" he grumbled. Luckily, the counters were opening now; he wanted to check in immediately but his inner voice told him to "take it slow" and to "act a bit refined." He recalled his old days again, when he had seen other passengers rushing to the counters to board. The tension on his face was replaced by a smug grin because he didn't have to hurry; he would just check in at the business counter and casually swagger to the CIP lounge.

The Spirit of Red Carpet

He waited for a few moments before edging forward. There were two people in front of him at the business counter. Not a problem. This won't take long, he thought. He stepped onto the red carpet to wait and looked more closely at the passengers in front of him. The first in line was a foreign man in his 60s dressed in shabby clothes, which did not fit the stereotype of a business class passenger. Fortunately, the other passenger, the woman in front of him, was chic and elegant, obviously, someone quite wealthy. She must be a senior manager or owner of a company, he thought. He looked at her Gucci suitcases and then to his own which looked like they'd been trampled underfoot at the Pamplona bull run, causing him to feel a little inadequate. Then he noticed that the line wasn't moving and saw that the delay was because the shabby guy was taking forever. He started to get annoyed and then saw that the economyclass counters were now empty. An attendant called out, "You can check in here." The woman in front of him was on the phone, unaware. Just for a moment, he considered stepping to the other side but remained on the red carpet. The attendant called out again, "Sir, you can check in here." He turned his head as if he'd just spotted a squirrel and was trying to track it. The shabby guy finally finished checking in, and the woman stepped forward, handing the check-in clerk her ticket. Meanwhile, he continued to avoid catching the attendant's eye. Thank god, she didn't take too long. After he had checked in, he proceeded quickly to the security check. "Hope it goes smooth from here" he said to himself. He couldn't understand how such a simple incident had been so teethgrindingly annoying; the sense of inadequacy that he felt while waiting at the check-in counter remained. Even the thought of the CIP lounge with its ambiance of the casino at Monte Carlo and the good food didn't help relieve his tension or lift his spirits.

2.

Why are people willing to hand over a bunch of extra money just to sit in the front row of a flight that lasts only a couple of hours, and yet think twice about spending $15 on a burger and fries at the airport? Or why would they board the plane ahead of their fellow passengers instead of enjoying the lounge? Why won't they step off their precious red carpet when they have the chance of a faster check-in at an economy check-in counter?

Now clearly, airline companies give business passengers more than just a free meal, a seat that's five centimetres wider and a drink of orange juice. When they enter the airport from a separate gate or step onto the red carpet before checking in, the serotonin molecule gang leap into action, pulsing through their blood and they feel just fantastic – a feeling so good it makes them want more and more of it. This is the reason they rush to board the plane before everybody instead of relaxing in the lounge. They take their front seat just like an artist on the stage.

The envious glances of the economy passengers as they go down the aisle make them feel superior. It is even better if they run into someone they know – at that very moment they are blown away by serotonin. The delight of sending them off to their back seats after a short conversation is priceless. 'Nice to see you again, now run along dear boy, I've my free New York Times to read.'

Of course, we can't allow these feelings to be obvious — in modern societies these feelings must hide in the shadows. It is not acceptable to talk about the pleasures brought on by serotonin. Most people can detect this type of motivation in others but shy away from admitting that they are prone to it themselves and would deny this reality if challenged.

3.

Equality has been one of the basic priorities of mankind since the Age of Enlightenment. There have been fierce struggles, wars and revolutions to overcome inequalities based on race, religion and nationality. Several monarchies and empires swirled down the plug hole before the Universal Declaration of Human Rights stated that "All human beings are born free and equal in dignity and rights."

But this doesn't explain why are we trying to prove that we're smarter, prettier or more successful than one another despite this powerful discourse on equality? What is the source of this irresistible desire for high status? Why the yearning to dominate others? Do we want equality among others while we are superior to them? Perhaps we need to search for answers to these questions, again, in our primitive brain.

4.

In ancient times, when people couldn't save money for rainy days of course; they saved surplus energy and turned it into social power to help them survive. That was how individual status was decided in the hierarchy. In fact, this wasn't planned; every individual had to learn who had their back and who might make off with their silver the minute they fell asleep. That's why hierarchies evolved.

Those with bigger muscles, the fleet of foot or people as agile as modern day Chinese acrobats, all acquired certain rights such as choosing the best part of the catch or selecting a mate.

In addition, when hunting, they had the power to send men with a lower status into danger. This was far from neighbourly but the point was to transfer their superior genes to the next generation. Therefore, serotonin was the basis of the survival structure and, once again, thanks to serotonin, the elimination of weak genes, the effects of which contributed to the continuation of mankind. Three cheers for serotonin!

Today, social status continues to be vital for our primitive brains. From keeping up with the Joneses, to holidaying on a cruise ship with more funnels than any other cruisers at the office, despite all our knowledge of how unethical it is to attempt to dominate others, status still matters. For instance, when watching the series, Game of Thrones, you would not approve Cersei Lannister's sneaky plans, plots and ruthless decisions because on a rational level they conflict with the values that matter to you.[4] However, on another level, which is governed by your conniving primitive brain, you probably hope that she retains her power and status, no matter what. This is the reason why the audience is pleased when Cersei wins back his power at the expense of hundreds of people who are burned alive.

5.

Elevated status not only results in being considered important or being treated as having value, it also makes our lives easier by bringing us money, freedom and comfort. Even today, high status people still have priority over resources and privileges. These privileges include free public service, special waiting lounges in airports, front seats at concerts and the best restaurant tables.

Now, you'll probably say that these are not important to you. You may even consider it foolish to try to get the best table at a restaurant because you know that it is not a matter of life or death. Yet, our primitive brain doesn't approach the situation in a rational way. It constantly checks our social status and becomes alarmed at the slightest negative development.

Therefore, your perspective changes when you are not given a good table, and your reactions in these situations are so disproportionate to the actual benefits you would otherwise receive. Status anxiety is created by feelings of neglect and a feeling of being slighted takes hold and urges you to compensate for these negative emotions. In short, feelings will override logic and those apparently trivial things will compel you to cut off your nose to spite your face.

6.

As a matter of fact, status anxiety is not only evoked by situations of humiliation or neglect. When someone that we consider to be our equivalent becomes prominent in a situation, the same kind of anxiety appears, even though there are no direct implications for us personally. For example, if we are short and live with people of a similar height, we would not normally be concerned with height.

However, if only one of the people in the group was to grow taller, our primitive brain would immediately become alarmed and we would feel the clutches of jealousy and dissatisfaction that we would not be able to make sense of – when in fact our height remained exactly the same and we didn't become shorter by even a single millimeter.[5]

We usually compare ourselves with reference groups when we assess our status. Reference groups generally consist of people who we grew up with, our colleagues and friends. We desire to be in a better position than them in order to deem ourselves successful. On the other hand, their accomplishments can, in many circumstance, lead to serious anxiety on our part because this indicates a weakening of our relative status. If Nerdy Norm from High School now runs his own software company with branches in 20 states, and you're still stacking shelves into the wee small hours at Walmart, you are bound to feel wounded.

Yet, we can't express our emotions about this openly because society would not approve of this anxiety. A similar case is also valid for the feelings negativity experienced by people in the reference group. If Lance Sterling, the boy most likely to make it 'big style' in college, ends up with his uninsured hardware store being ripped to pieces by a force 5 hurricanes, we are secretly pleased. Our primitive brain rewards such developments instantly but, of course, schadenfreude is unacceptable. Therefore, we mask our true feelings and might even shed a bucket of crocodile tears over our colleague's misfortune.

'Not me, buddy' I hear you say. Well, you may be different. However, if you observe closely, you will be able to trace this tendency in almost everyone around you. Now, imagine a group of women who have gathered for five o'clock tea. The host is serving tea and guests are chatting. One of the women starts talking about her son's success at college. She goes on about his scholarship, grades and every award from Best adderup in math class to the Nobel Prize for Clever Clogging. How do you think the other women might react to this?

• They would stop and slavishly give their undivided attention to what she is saying

• They would shower her with questions to find out more details about her son's accomplishments

• They would pretend to be listening to her with a smile on their face as rigid as an ironing board.

Which of the above do you think is most likely to happen?

Now, let's imagine a different situation. In this case, a woman is talking about her daughter who is being cheated on by her husband. What would be the reactions in this case? Would the women stay indifferent to this story or would they want to go into every little detail of the situation?

Of course, I am not saying that we need to underestimate the successes of others or get pleasure out of their suffering. I am simply trying to bring your attention to our evolutionary instincts which force us to make social comparisons and induce desires of superiority.

Let's consider the source of this instinct and its implications for our social lives.

7.

I am inviting you to evaluate a study which was conducted by American researchers in order to explain the influence of social status on self-confidence.[6] In a zoo, researchers place the leader of a group of gorillas behind a oneway mirrored window so that members of the group can't see the leader, however, the leader can see the other members. The alpha gorilla, totally unaware of the situation, performs his usual antics in a show of strength and intimidation. Initially, the alpha gorilla goes into a rage when the others pay him no attention. He shrieks and bangs wildly on the window. However, after just a few days, the ongoing indifference has totally destroyed his self-confidence. He is now unable to show any superiority even after the window is removed. He becomes insignificant and is treated with lack of respect.

Adam Smith summarizes this situation in his work, The Theory of Moral Incidents,[7] "The rich man fully enjoys his wealth because the world's attention and admiration comes along with his riches. The poor man, on the contrary, feels ashamed of his poverty because it makes him invisible among people. Nobody notices of him on his way to work and back home. Being among people or being isolated makes no difference at all. In both cases, he is obscure and invisible while the rich man is in front of the eyes of the whole world. Everybody wants to get a glance of him; everything about him is met with enthusiasm."

This research and the analysis demonstrate that we need the approval of others for self-confidence. This is quite concerning, nevertheless, this is how our primitive brain functions, whether we like it or not. Serotonin, which is triggered by the praises of others, makes us feel fantastic, while cortisol, which is released when we are humiliated, evokes a fierce anxiety that could shatter our lives. This situation is explained in the work of William James, *The Principles of Psychology*:[8] "If it was physically possible to set a guilty person free while ensuring a total social isolation and neglect, this would absolutely be the cruelest method of punishment."

In the modern world, even though this type of punishment is not possible, failure hangs on by a thread; the smallest mistake might have huge consequences. Going downhill, that is to say, the thought of not being able to release serotonin any more, creates a ferocious and a detrimental fear which can consume us. We feel this anxiety deep down even though we have no knowledge of hormones. A friend ignoring us by not returning our phone call or even being uninterested in our social media posts may affect us deeply. Self-pride is secured as long as serotonin is released but loss of self-respect may be underway in the absence of it.

This explains why, all our lives, we continuously strive to prove to others how valuable we are. We yearn for attention; compliments and admiration are extremely important to us. Although we claim that, "I don't care what others think about me," we will be all ears we will listen to someone who is talking about us for hours.

Shortcuts to Serotonin

8.

After reading this, you might ask whether there is an easier way to get hold of serotonin. Certainly, there are short cuts and, as with dopamine, we resort to these short cuts quite frequently. What are these shortcuts? Let's begin with the most innocent one.

Gossip

'Four horses cannot overtake the tongue,' runs the Chinese proverb. Gossip is forbidden in all religions and is seen as one of the biggest sins. But this is difficult to take on board when you're hanging around the water cooler during break, dishing the dirt with like-minded souls. This is because gossip provides indescribable joy with the serotonin it generates. Do you think this is an exaggeration? Please picture the people around you. Have some managed to lose weight, give up smoking, or quit alcohol? Your answer would probably be "Yes." Have you seen anyone who stopped gossiping? To tell the truth, I haven't.

Now, think of a scenario where there is a medium-sized family business. It is noon time. The boss enters his office, acting like a grizzly bear with a hangover. He asks his secretary to get the production manager to his office immediately. After he enters, shouts and insults are heard. What is the first thing the production manager is likely to do after he leaves the office? Yes, he's likely to go to one his colleagues and start gossiping, saying how narrow minded, ignorant and rude the boss is. His colleague will probably agree with him and say the boss does not have the skills to run a company and could not even find his ass using both hands.

In fact, this conversation is neither unique or unusual; this scenario is being played out countless times. So, why then do people never get tired of telling and listening to the same things? The fact is that gossip is basically an effort to weaken the dignity and reputation of this unpopular boss. It is not important whether this is achieved because the primitive brain is not able to gauge this. What matters is that this kind of conversation triggers a large amount of serotonin thereby creating a temporary relief for water cooler gossips with far too much time on their hands.

What about the other employees? Naturally, they leap onto the gossip bandwagon with wild abandon. No way are they going to miss out on a serotonin fest.

You may conclude that gossip is good as it provides relief for people, however, there is actually a dangerous side to it. Imagine you have an antidepressant that you may take as much of as you please, which you have been doing since you were very young, and you've been doing this without any breaks for your entire life. Then someone tells you that this is not good for you. Would you be able to give up this habit easily? Unfortunately, it is very difficult, if not impossible.

In summary, gossiping is a sneaky habit. Even though it brings a considerable amount of relief and happiness in the beginning, it harms our social relations and dignity in the medium or long-term. Just like other short cuts, it destroys the natural flow of happy chemicals, therefore, moves us away from "real happiness."[9]

Those Who Butter Up

It is the early years of my consulting business. I am restructuring a family company, and all the managers are trying to support me as much as they can. However, Tom is an executive assistant that I am in constant dispute with. As I attempt to point out the problems, he puts forward a rosy picture. One day, during a meeting with the CEO, I mention that Tom is lying and is trying to steer the management in the wrong direction. The CEO smiles at me and says, "I know. He is lying but he is doing it well."

Despite our knowledge of their insincerity, we want such people around us because they function like a happiness factory that help us to release serotonin even at the most difficult times and therefore create a relief for us. Moreover, when we are happy, they supplement our joy with the surplus serotonin they provide. It is quite difficult to reject their compliments even though we find it very disturbing when they butter up others.

Brands

Today, brands promise consumers that if they use their products or services they will be transformed into the people they dream of being. A spray or two of perfumed chemicals in the armpits, for example, virtually guarantees to turn men into babe magnets.

Very few people can isolate themselves from the magical world of brands even though people generally claim to be unaffected by these messages. The result is a world full of girls who think a shampoo containing jojoba oil, essence of avocado and the bark of the baobab tree, will help get a date with their Prince Charming. A person buying the same cough drops as a celebrity starts feeling popular and cool, despite his hacking cough. People borrow from friends or strain the upper limits of their credit card limits to buy designer footwear, get the latest mobile phone or buy a second or third handbag. None of these purchases are based on need – they are merely to attract attention, recognition, admiration and approval.

In summary, we pay a fortune for branded products because they evoke feelings of status, prestige and social power, which are, in effect, short cuts. That is to say, we go beyond our means just for the sake of a few doses of serotonin.[10]

Social Media

One of the authors of Fast Company, E. B. Boyd, describes serotonin as the 'secret sauce of Facebook.'[11] According to Boyd, serotonin triggered by that tiny 'like' button lies behind the outstanding success story of Facebook. Of course, that magical sauce is not a secret anymore because the 'like' button is now ubiquitous across all social media platforms.

Can we describe social media usage as an addiction? Internet users in the US spend an average of 1.7 hours a day on social media. In Turkey it is 2.5 hours, in Brazil 3.3, and Lord knows what's going on in the Philippines, where they spend almost 4 hours on this!

If we conducted a survey right now and asked people why they spend time on social media, do you think 'fess up, saying stuff like 'to follow my friends, to check my status, to gather likes, to pamper my ego?' More likely responses would tend toward the rational: '...to learn new things, to communicate with friends.' All these were possible in the BFB era (Before FaceBook), in the olden days of 2004 when we spent around forty minutes a day on the Internet.

Today, many people cling to their mobile phones like Koala Bears cling to Eucalyptus trees and cannot bear to part with them even when visiting the bathroom. They check their likes every five minutes after each post. You might have thought that a few likes wouldn't trigger much serotonin but every molecule counts when it comes to serotonin.

Antidepressants and Cocaine

It is an obvious fact that happiness brought on by antidepressants and cocaine is artificial so we won't go into details here. Just on a technical note, antidepressants, which are called SSRIs (selective serotonin re-uptake inhibitors), slow down the absorption of serotonin thus leading to an increased amount in the blood. Cocaine creates a similar effect and scales up the serotonin in addition to dopamine.[12]

9.

You can immediately ask this question, "What is wrong with creating happiness by using a short cut?" I mean, shortcuts are good, aren't they? Cutting twenty minutes off our daily commute would surely be seen as a good thing. But only if you avoided risks, like speeding, or recklessly overtaking to achieve your goal. And that's the problem — serotonin carries a number of negative aspects: Serotonin;

• Leads to high levels of addiction

• Creates feeling of happiness which do not last

• Is required in ever-increasing amounts to replicate the desired effect (more compliments, more admiration, higher dosage...)

• Creates a dangerously attractive virtual world which detracts from reality

• In the long term, harms our health and seriously damages our social relations

Not much good news there then.

How would you rate the sincerity of relationships established through social media or the comments and the likes that a post gathers? I have approximately five thousand friends on Facebook, probably 95% of which I wouldn't recognize if I saw them in person. Moreover, I believe most people click the 'like' button or leave comments on my posts without even reading the content. I am sure this is similar to your social media experience.

While we are aware of all this we still can't resist social media because of our desire to experience the joy that is induced by serotonin. Comments that are full of praise escalate our morale in our struggle with the problems of modern life. Momentary escapes from reality and the comfort of the virtual world is soothing. As a result, we become addicted slowly and end up spending a considerable amount of our time on social media.

The pleasure we get from the likes and comments diminish over time and we start saying, that social media is not as much fun as it once was. Why is that? It is simply because our serotonin threshold has increased. That is to say, as time passes, we need more and more likes, and more exaggerated comments and compliments in order to trigger the same amount of serotonin. For example, when you first start using Facebook, thirty likes will please you, whereas this amount wouldn't be satisfying after a while.

When you have less than thirty likes, you find yourself checking who liked and who didn't react to your posts. You might even come up with scenarios like, "Why didn't Frank like this? Maybe it's because of my comment about his nose being bigger than a ripe mango the other day?" You know this is a ridiculous thought but you can't get it out of your mind until you reach forty or fifty likes at which point the shape of Frank's nose and his reaction to your comments about it, cease to matter. Social media is fun again – until the next time you are dissatisfied with the number of likes.

Within this framework, we can describe the "serotonin threshold" as the point where our brain starts triggering serotonin. Our primitive brain forces us to develop and strive for improvement by continuously trying to raise this threshold. First it was thirty likes, then fifty and then a hundred, thereby making the release of serotonin increasingly difficult every day.

We often hear how Hollywood stars succumb to depression when they lose their fame. This might sound illogical to many; it is difficult to understand the unhappiness of these people who lead extremely wealthy lives. However, from the joy.ology perspective, the situation is pretty clear. Years of fame and attention raise the serotonin threshold of actors and pop stars to very high levels. These people, who get accustomed to such a life, start finding it really difficult to trigger serotonin once they lose their popularity.

As the primitive brain demands more and more, what they have doesn't suffice to make them happy and they may end up trying to fill this serotonin gap with drugs. Usually, celebrities find themselves in a vicious cycle and the fans fail to understand the situation when they read the news that these stars have committed suicide.

The same is valid for politicians, bosses and top managers. These people expect respect and subordination from others because of their status. As their expectations are met, they feel great because of the released serotonin. Yet, the primitive brain, after a short while, raises the serotonin threshold and leads them to strive more and more for higher status.

However, expanding the business or being promoted is not very easy and this is the point where the "Butter Up Team" (typically comprising a Chief Sycophant, a Deputy Sycophant and four hangers on) steps in to fill the serotonin gap. These people with their words and actions make their managers feel more valuable than they actually are. What happens then? Praise and compliments create an ever-increasing need and the serotonin threshold heightens more rapidly than before. After a while, their egos hit the ceiling and they start to believe they can walk on water.

However, such a self-perception can no longer be supported by solid reason and strong criteria. As a result, saving appearances becomes their basic priority. They feel their smallest mistake will destroy them and lead to the loss of all attention. That's why they become extra sensitive to criticism and can't tolerate it. In an effort to mask their fragile and sensitive psychological state they adopt an extremely hash approach and pattern of behavior. Besides, their personality becomes like a balloon continuously losing air which creates a desperate need for more compliments to inflate it. They become more in need of praise than ever. It takes a while to end up with only the "Butter Up Team" around them and they go under these people's control, who have nothing to offer but empty compliments.

10.

If we could function only with our rational side, we wouldn't be so obsessed with people's criticisms and gossip, and again we wouldn't be addicted to compliments. Our own thoughts would prevail and we could tell those who would criticise us to go boil their heads. However, whether we like it or not, this is how we are. This is how our brain functions. But at least now we know that;

• Happiness that is reached the easy way is not sustainable.

• Taking advantage of our brain's weaknesses has rather heavy implications.

Now, we know what not to do, let's do what we should do!

The Serotonin Experience

11.

Einstein, the world-renowned scientist who seemed always to be having a bad hair day, is preparing for a science meeting that will be held outside the university. His assistant sees that he is still wearing a lab coat with more ballpoint pens in his top pocket than any scientist could possibly use in fifty years and suggests that he wears something else to the meeting. Einstein says, "Never mind...nobody knows us there." Then, over time, Einstein's popularity grows. Again, just before a meeting, his assistant suggests that he changes his lab coat, or at least loose some of the pens and asks, "Is this how you are going to attend the meeting?" This time, Einstein says, "Never mind... those who know me already know how I am."

What determines our social status? Is it our knowledge, the value we create, the contribution we make to society? Or is it our wind powered ecowatch, the computer on wheels that is our current automobile of choice, or the Michelin starred restaurants eat at? First, we have to make a clear distinction between those in order to reach a healthy serotonin experience and sustainable happiness?

Rule Number 1: Why should people respect you? What do you want to be remembered for? Answer these questions before you go into a status struggle.

12.

Jose Mujica, or Pepe as he was widely known, was the former president of Uruguay. He now lives on a rundown farm and donates most of his salary to the poor. He works in the fields with his wife. His bodyguard is Manuela, a three legged dog and his residence – a farm house. This is how he summarizes serotonin addiction and its consequences:

'We have created a huge heap of redundant needs. We buy something and then throw it away. It is our lives that we actually waste because when we buy something we pay not only with money but also with the time that we spent making that money. Yet, you can't buy life. Life flows away; it is just horrible to waste your life and lose your freedom.'

'When I ask people, "Money or freedom?" their answer is usually "Both." We tend to believe that money brings freedom. However, we can't see that as long as our expectations rise and we are not content with what we have, we will never feel rich enough regardless of how much money we make'

Approximately two hundred and fifty years ago, Jean Jacques Rousseau, in his work, Discourse on Equality, said this:[13] 'Wealth does not necessarily mean possessing too much. It rather means having what we want. We become poor when we want something and can't afford it, regardless of our means. We become rich when we are content with what we have, regardless of how little we have.'

Compared to the lives of the vast majority of our forebears, living in a cardboard box would be considered luxurious by comparison. We live in unimaginable wealth and abundance compared to those of approximately one hundred years ago, who strove to make ends meet under extreme hardship. Yet, in spite of all this abundance, we are in a relentless struggle for more and this drags us to a level of unhappiness unprecedented in the history of mankind.

What should we do?

According to William James, psychology professor at Harvard, "When we struggle for more, we ascribe all our pride and self-respect to what we do and that is the main reason for our unhappiness. This is basically why failure is devastating. It is our goals that determine what is failure or victory. A rise in expectations causes an increase the risks of frustration."[14] That is why an old couple living in a village on their retirement salary can lead a happier life than a businessman who resides in his splendid mansion in the New York but can't sleep for his failure anxiety.

And the businessman can die with indescribable sorrow and pain while he has so much more in his possession compared to the old couple. Therefore, we have two options: We either fuel our dopamine and serotonin addiction by raising our goals continuously or keep our expectations under control.

Rule Number 2: Review your expectations or as Mujica puts it: "Open space for life."

13.

Imagine a graduation ceremony. Your son graduates at the top of his college and he is going to give a speech. You and your spouse are in the front row to watch him. The ceremony starts and the Dean speaks. Then, your son's name is announced. He stands up and starts walking towards the stage. The serotonin triggered by your brain at that moment fills you with an amazing feeling of joy and pride. Your son finishes his speech by extending his special thanks to teachers and his parents. The serotonin in you and your son's blood hits peak levels, further strengthening the bond between the two of you. You want to hug your son breathless after the ceremony and meet all the people involved in his success, shaking their hands until there's a risk of their arms dislocating at the shoulder. You feel that all of these people, whom you have never met, are like close friends.

The Unifying Power of Serotonin

Alert readers will have spotted the inconsistency here. In all previous examples, the discriminating quality of serotonin was emphasized. In traditional structures where competition is prominent, when someone gets ahead, others feel like failures. But, what if we create work environments in which cooperation prevails rather than competition? Then, can the accomplishments play a unifying role, just as it did in the graduation ceremony? Can we, in other words, reverse the traditional function of serotonin? Why not? In his work "7 Habits of Highly Effective People," Stephen R. Covey describes this approach as "Win/Win." According to Covey, Win/Win represents a mentality of a continuous and mutual benefit in all kinds of human interaction. The Win/Win approach requires that all solutions should be beneficial and satisfying for both parties.

The thought of abundance underlies the Win/Win approach.[15] That is to say, there is enough for everybody. However, the majority operates with the "Mentality of Scarcity." People with this mentality find it difficult to share fame and success with others. When someone other than themselves succeeds, they feel like something has been taken away from them. On the other hand, abundance mentality, takes its source from a deep notion of individual value and a feeling of security. Such mentality views the sharing of prestige, fame, success and gain as both possible and highly desirable.

Rule Number 3: Move with Win-Win perspective

I am certainly aware that all of this is easier said than done. It's easy in the same way that playing the flute is as easy as blowing across a hole in a metal tube while waggling your fingers over a bunch of other holes. Sadly, this will not be enough for you to master Mozart's Flute Concerto No. 1 in G Major. Your efforts to improve the serotonin experience[16] will reduce the ups and downs that stem from it, however we cannot eliminate it entirely. On the other hand, as long as they are within certain limits, such ups and downs enrich our lives. Especially, when there are other hormones that rush to our help and substitute the serotonin gap during our declines.

I am referring to ENDORPHINE and OXYTOCIN.

Let's have a closer look at these two hormones which, in times of need, jump on their trusty steeds and ride to our aid, strengthening us, make us feel good and safe, protecting our health and enhancing our happiness with each passing day.

PART SIX

Yes, I feel good

Endorphin: Happiness Brought by Pain

Through the blood, sweat, and tears, many runners experience euphoria, a feeling of being invincible, a reduced state of discomfort or pain, and even a loss in sense of time while running. So where does euphoria experience come from, and what makes athletes push themselves for miles? Long-duration exercise releases endorphins, which have a morphine-like effect on the body and therefore is responsible for the feelings of euphoria. Besides, endorphin not only masks physical pain but also makes us feel good by reducing the cortisol level in our blood.

In this chapter, we'll take a closer look at endorphin and explain in detail the changes that occur in our brains and bodies following endorphin release. When you complete this chapter, you will consider starting to work out or even decide to make it an integral part of your life.

He slumped in front of his computer like a zombie who's spent all night haunting the living. He should have been finalizing that brilliant report — the one that seemed dazzling to his mind but that a massive writer's block prevented him from producing before he left the office. He stared at the screen and the screen stared back at him. It was already 10 pm and he had descended to trying to out-stare a monitor! Nor was he any closer to finishing. He couldn't organize his thoughts, but it was like trying to herd cats with a fly swatter. This, he thought, was because of the 'incident' earlier in the day. Long story cut short: Friends he trusted had betrayed him. Bummer. And these were friends he had helped a lot too. Double bummer. 'This shouldn't have happened' he said to himself. He'd been so humiliated by his boss that his capacity for report writing had disappeared in less time than it took Usain Bolt to cover 100 meters and the time available for completing the report disappeared at roughly the same rate. Failure to make a blockbusting presentation the next day suggested career suicide. Maybe this was part of a conspiracy to get him fired. 'Surely not' he mused, 'If that was their intention, the conspirators would have come up with something more challenging than this: Telling the MD I had pissed in the water cooler, maybe. Normally he could have written such a report hanging upside down from a bridge blindfolded.'

Then, he got annoyed at himself. He offered himself a challenge: 'If you don't focus, this child's play will finish you off,' he shouted at his shaving mirror. He really tried hard to get over his worries and fully concentrate on his work but he just couldn't. In his mind, it was as if the report had been shredded in a cross-shedder — the kind that shreds horizontally and vertically — and he was trying to reconstitute the tiny shredded squares, blindfolded, with a glue stick, after 12 G&Ts. No matter how hard he tried to unscramble the letters, sentences and paragraphs, he just found himself staring at his computer screen's blinking cursor. Why was it even blinking he thought, couldn't the damned thing just stay still? Then he realized that an unblinking cursor would be the stupidest idea since the wind powered draught excluder. It couldn't be found without calling in a graphics engineer at $50 an hour.

Suddenly, he stood up. All this talk of cursors was driving him batty. He had to get some fresh air, 'Half an hour's walk might help' he murmured. 'Jogging would be even better' he said to himself — or if things didn't improve, throwing himself over a bridge. Certainly, whenever he found himself on the losing end of an argument with his wife — more frequent than rain in the Amazon basin. — he would go out and jog to unscramble his thoughts ad dissipate his anger. The clock was ticking, and far too loud for that matter. Did clocks have volume controls? Yet he couldn't write one single sentence. He puled on his running gear and practically threw himself out the door. He huffed and puffed his way toward the beach but gloom surrounded him like Inland Revenue inspectors round a tax dodger. Then he saw lights in the window of a restaurant up ahead. Suddenly, he wanted to drink something a lot stronger than a medium dry sherry and in quantities fit to fell a yak. To forget everything. He imagined getting so drunk that he'd get home and try to take his trousers off over his head before going to bed. 'I am not letting anyone do this to me' he said to himself and lifted the pace a notch. He tried to expunge the negative thoughts from his mind by taking long, deep breaths in through his ears and out through the top of his head like he'd read about in a book of advanced Buddhist meditations but this proved beyond him.

He wanted to scream in the key of F# minor (was he going mad?) but what good would that do? The police rarely take kindly to joggers belting along the side of the sea uttering tonsil-rattling yells. He'd probably get arrested for disturbing the peace, or put in a straight jacket. He started running faster and the urge to scream subsided. After a while, he felt a kind of spontaneous, effortless relief. He no longer felt under pressure; his mind had become clear. His mind flooded with ideas for the report. 'I can't let this moment go,' he said to himself. He went to a nearby café and asked a waiter for pen and paper.

He began to write what had been revealed to him. Soon, he had covered four sheets of paper with closely packed script. Now, he could go home and input what he had written to his computer. He felt so at ease, joyful even, because he had just nailed it. He left the cafe floating on air, walked for a while and started running back home, happier than he'd ever been before.

1.

Most of the time, when we are worried about something and unable to express it openly, we snack. It's a form of relaxation. In such cases, a slice of cake the size of a pizza or a heavy dessert like baklava usually hits the spot. Shopping is another option; purchasing popularly branded products has a magical, though short-lived effect. To ease the intensity of our negative feelings, we either mount an assault on the fridge or thrash our credit cards until they squeal. We just can't help ourselves, even though we are well aware of the later regrets.

Good news: There are better alternatives to stuffing ourselves stupid or binge-shopping for the latest gadgets and gizmos. When depressed we don't have to respond to our primitive brain's urge to 'do something' by dopamine that is triggered by cheeseburgers or by serotonin which is released by the desire to hit the local shopping mall with a Mastercard in one hand and a Platinum Visa in the other. You can be sure that endorphin which is triggered by a high pace walk or jogging at low tempo will make you feel far better (and cheaper) This is because our factory settings project energy that is gathered at moments of stress to be consumed either by fighting with the threat that is faced or by running away from it like a big sissy.[1] Our brain remains alarmed as long as the energy is not consumed and urges us to store more. Occasional work out or exercise after stressful moments provides a relief by breaking this vicious cycle and protects us from the many-headed monster of stress.

I advised a friend of mine who was going through a financially challenging time to take a 30-minute walk twice a day. He took my advice and even increased the duration of his walks and later joined a fitness club. He goes for a walk anytime he feels the desire to eat a box of cream crackers or put four spoons of sugar in his coffee, or even nibble on something. This lifestyle choice helped him through his crisis without any health problems. Later on, sport became an integral part of his life. If he wasn't kayaking he was pole-vaulting and if he wasn't pole-vaulting he was white water rafting. His sole motive for exercising now goes beyond just reducing the pressure of stress to clearing his mind, thinking healthier, feeling better and staying happy.

2.

I am sure that you would have witnessed similar stories around you. Stories of people who has recorded a major turnaround in their lives through exercise. Or, is it the other way around? That said, most of us could recount as many tales about colleagues who made resolutions about exercising, became members of fitness clubs and began to do sports with great motivation only to quit after a short time. To which group do you belong?

Most of us plan to exercise. Some of us even carry the plan out. But we often avoid saying out loud how long we'll stick to that plan. This is because we usually view sports as a means of losing weight and improving our physique, in other words, of turning ourselves into babe or dude magnets, hyper-attractive to the opposite sex. However, such transformations take more time and effort than most of us can muster and our motivation runs away faster than the sand in an egg timer. Research by David K. Inglewdew of Bangor University on 252 respondents, revealed that exercising which with the sole objective of losing weight or improving the figure don't last and fail to become habitual.[2] So we must find a way to work out which generates more happiness than torturing ourselves to lose a couple of pounds.

Such a mindset transformation requires the establishment of a mental three benchmark 'exercise-health-happiness' relationship in order to achieve our goals (and so defeat the alternative three benchmark relationship of couch potato, middle age spread and despair). Of course, this is not so easy to do, since most of us are conditioned with a belief in the "no pain, no gain" approach. This convinces us that the only way to achieve our aim is to go beyond our limits. This assumption has led to downplaying the benefits of easy walks and jogging, thereby making them of less use because we see them as being a bit soppy — activities for flower arrangers and soft shoe shuffle dancers. However, we need to drop such thoughts if exercise is to become an integral part of our lives. We can overcome the bottlenecks preventing our happiness and create the lifestyle we desire by taking half an hour walks, three to four times a week.

Not convinced? I hope the scientific research findings in this chapter change your whole perspective on exercise.

3.

First of all, let's try to answer this: 'How much does exercise affect our happiness and health?' I would like to share the results of research carried out by James Blumenthal of Duke University in order to compare the influence of antidepressants and exercise in the treatment of depression.

James Blumenthal and his team divided one hundred and fifty-six patients, suffering from depression, into three groups in order to find out how regular exercise influenced treatment for depression. The first group was treated with Zoloft, an antidepressant from the SSRI group, for six weeks. The second group, instead of medical treatment, followed an exercise plan of jogging or walking for three times a week that increased their heart rates by 75-85%. The third group was exposed to both medical treatment and the exercise plan simultaneously. Patients in all the three groups improved significantly and half of the patients were discharged. The initial findings showed that regular exercise is as essential as medication in the treatment of depression. The patients were re-examined after six months in order to assess the long-term effects of the treatments. The findings were rather astonishing, even for Blumenthal. 38% of the patients in the Zoloft group had to restart the treatment while this figure was only eight percent for patients who exercised. Regular exercise proved to be four times more effective than medication in the treatment of depression.[3]

What about antidepressants other than Zoloft? A group of German researchers led by Andreas Broocks conducted research to assess the effects of the antidepressant, Clomipramine in comparison to exercise. The research was carried out on a total of 46 patients, for a period of sixteen weeks. The research findings found regular exercise to be more effective than Clomipramine treatment.[4]

Madhukar Trivedi, director of the Research Programme on Mental Health Disorder at Texas University, put seventeen patients who showed no improvement during a four-month antidepressant treatment into an exercise program. Nine of these patients dropped out of the program, as many do, while five of the remaining eight patients were recovered and discharged. The numbers in this survey were low but results are groundbreaking; exercise had made recovery possible where medical treatment failed.[5]

Trevedi repeated this research in 2011, on a group of 126 patients. In this study, patients who had used SSRI antidepressants for at least two months without any improvement were put on an exercise programme. 29.5% of the patients recovered fully at the end of the fourth month of the treatment.[6]

You may think that because these studies were conducted in controlled conditions and that things are different in real life. Let's continue with some examples from a business environment to overcome such doubts.

In 2004, a group of academicians from Leeds Metropolitan University conducted a full day observation of a group of employees in a company. At the end of the day, the employees were asked whether they could complete their work on time, their experience with their colleagues and how they felt. 65% of respondents in the study (a total of two hundred and ten people) scored higher on these three categories on the days they exercised. In other words, employees could establish better relations with their colleagues, use time more efficiently, were less prone to feeling like their only relief was to head butt the water cooler and felt more full of beans at the office even though they'd exercised at lunch time.

In another study, researchers monitored more than 2,000 cardiac patients in USA, France and Canada for more than a year. It was observed that patients who exercised 90-120 minutes per week showed less symptoms of stress.[7]

When we examined the annual reports of global companies, we can see that employees who do exercise have less health problems. For example, Northern Gas Company which introduced a routine exercise program claims that their employee-doctor visit rate dropped by 85%. Research conducted in General Electric, shows that the doctor-visit rate of the employees who became fitness club members decreased by 27% while the non-members rate increased by seventeen per cent. In other research conducted by Coca Cola at the end of the 90's, it was observed that the health expenses of the employees who attended the company exercise program were $500 less than the ones who did not attend.[8]

In addition to all the above, a broad scoped research carried out in Finland, covering 3,400 people, showed that people who exercised were less anxious, less depressed and less angry compared to people who didn't work out. Another research conducted in Germany on approximately 20,000 people reveals that people who work out regularly feel happier and enjoy life better, with little or no worries.[9]

Now, going back to the initial question: "How much does exercise affect our happiness and health?" Research findings tell us that:

• Regular exercise is effective in making, even, the depressed people happy.

• People who exercise not only feel good but also experience fewer health problems.

What about our mental performance?

The positive effects of exercise have been known for some time; its history dates back hundreds of years. For instance, Nietzsche viewed walking outdoors as one of life's blessings. He used to walk and take notes, whenever his fragile health allowed him to go out. He expressed his faith in walking, in his work, The Twilight of the Idols, "*A life without any physical activity is a true crime committed against the Holy Spirit. Thoughts during a walk have a real value*".[10]

Aristotle used to walk in the garden with his students while teaching. The "Peripatetic School" (*peripatetic means; traveler*), one of the four prominent schools of the ancient Greek philosophy, founded by Aristotle, took its name from this practice of walking. Besides, for Aristotle and his students, walking was not only a practice during lessons but also for reflecting and developing ideas.[11]

The latest research also supports Aristotle's practices and demonstrates us that regular exercise has a considerable influence on mental performance and the well-being of our brain. Let's quickly go through these studies.

Aristotle's Way of Developing Ideas

4.

Irish researchers applied a simple test to a group of college students to assess the influence of exercise on memory retention and loss. The students were shown slides with pictures and the names of 20 different people. Then, the names were covered and students asked to recall them. In the second phase of the test, half the students were exercised with cross trainers until they got tired while the others rested. The test was repeated by both groups till sufficient results had been collected. The group who worked out scored higher while there was no significant difference in the results of students who didn't exercise.[12]

Similar studies were conducted by many other researchers; results supported previous studies showing that exercising improves mental performance.

Charles Hillman and his team at Illinois University examined and compared the neural activities of the respondents' brains before and after a 20-minute workout. The test which was carried out via advanced imaging technologies revealed that even exercising for a short time had neurons in the brain leaping about like Mexican jumping beans.[13]

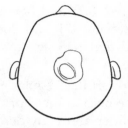 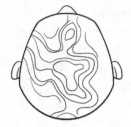

Brain After Sitting Quietly   **Brain After 20 Minutes Walk**

We know for a fact that mental performance increases after exercise. But, how long does this increase in performance last? Is it temporary or long term? Can we improve our mental performance by regular exercise?

Researchers at the Dartmouth College conducted research monitoring 54 adults between the ages of 18 and 34, who don't have a habit of exercising.[14] An extensive memory test was carried out on the respondents during their first visit to the lab. After which, the respondents were divided into two groups; the first group was introduced to a program which involved walking at a high pace for thirty minutes for four times a week while the second group continued their usual routine within this period. At the end of the fourth week when the memory test was repeated, respondents who exercised showed a significant improvement while there was no significant difference within the non-exercising group.

These results are important in showing us the long-term effect of exercising on our mental performance. In short, regular exercise improves the resilience of memory. What about memory loss? Can regular exercise slow down the rate of memory loss associated with aging?

Researchers at Edinburgh University collected detailed data from respondents aged 70 years and over. Details of their daily physical, mental and social activities and their brains were scanned with imaging devices. Three years later, when the scanning was repeated, less damage and less reduction in size was observed in the brains of the respondents who exercised intensively compared to others.[15] Also,

Denise Head and her team at the Washington University Alzheimer Research Center, discovered that regular exercising slows down the formation of Alzheimer, in an experiment involving 201 adults between the ages of 45 and 88.[16] Laura F. Defina and her team had monitored nineteen thousand adults between 1971 and 2009, for a period of twenty four years and observed that regular exercising reduces the risk of early dementia by 36%.[17]

In summary, we have solid data to support that regular exercising not only increases our mental performance both in the short and long term but it also reduces the risk of Alzheimer and early dementia by protecting our brain.

5.

Now let's see how working up a sweat creates this tremendous effect. The latest research using advanced imaging technologies revealed that new neuron formation in the hippocampus region is three times higher in brains of people who exercise than in the brains of people who don't work out. In other words, exercising speeds up the regeneration process of our memory function. Yet, as we emphasized earlier, neuronal connections are more important than their number. There is no point, for instance, in having 16 people in a football team if none can score a goal from the penalty spot with the goalkeeper lying bound and gagged in the dressing room; that is to say, new neuron formation is not sufficient by itself. What do we have to do besides physical exercise in order to strengthen our memory and protect ourselves from the risks that are brought by aging? Can mental exercise contribute in this respect?

One of the most convincing researches on this subject was conducted by Justin S. Rhodes, a professor of psychology at Beckman Institute.[18] In order to answer the questions above, Rhodes formed four separate groups using lab rats, each in different environments. In the first group's cage, labyrinths were used, making food acquisition challenging; mirrors and toys with little bells and balls were used to entertain them. The second cage was almost entirely empty except for the food. In the third cage, in addition to food, was placed a tiny running cylinder designed for the rats. The fourth cage had the same setting as the first group with the addition of the running cylinder.

Mental tests were done for all of the rats at the beginning of the study. Their brains were injected with a substance that would enable the scientists to monitor changes in their brains. Then, the rats started to live in the settings that were assigned to them. The rats in the first cage were living it up in their rich environment but didn't have it all their own way; they had to use their intelligence to work their way through mind-bogglingly complicated mazes and put all their efforts into reaching food. The rats in the second cage mooched about all day, busy doing nothing but eating — they were in fact the rodent equivalents of couch potatoes. The only entertainment for the third cage rats, except for the food, was the running wheel. The rats in the fourth cage had the same activities as the rats in the first one with the addition of the running wheel.

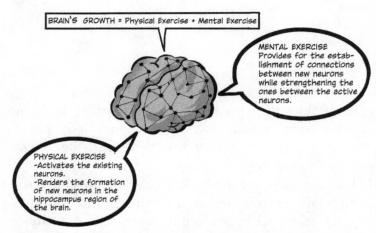

BRAIN'S GROWTH = Physical Exercise + Mental Exercise

MENTAL EXERCISE Provides for the establishment of connections between new neurons while strengthening the ones between the active neurons.

PHYSICAL EXERCISE
-Activates the existing neurons.
-Renders the formation of new neurons in the hippocampus region of the brain.

The Role of Physical and Mental Exercise in Brain Growth

Later on, the rats were re-tested and changes in their brains scanned with advanced imaging devices; the results were gobsmacking to say the least. No change was observed in the brains of the rats in the first cage. Contrary to expectations, a rich environment, diversity of the toys and mental activities had almost no influence on brain progress. According to Rhodes, only one factor made a difference: the running cylinder. The rats which had a running cylinder in their cage scored higher on mental tests regardless of the conditions they were exposed to and had healthier brains. Although the rats in the first cage were content, their setting didn't help them to get smarter as long as they didn't exercise because there was no facility for that. The rats in the fourth cage got the highest scores from the tests.

Then, the running cylinders were removed from the cages and the test was repeated, one month later. The rats that engaged in-both physical and mental exercise scored almost the same, on the other hand, the significant drop was observed in the group with physical exercise.

To sum up, the results of the experiment revealed that:

• Mental exercise alone (first cage) made almost no difference to the brain's growth or performance.

• Although physical exercise increases mental performance in the short term (third cage), it has to be supported by mental exercise, in order to attain long lasting results (forth cage).

6.

Mankind has found ways to trigger dopamine and serotonin by deceiving the brain with shortcuts ranging from eating high calorie food to swallowing antidepressants like M&Ms. These actions help us reach 'easy happiness' in times of need, even though they create serious problems in the long run.

Is this possible for endorphin too? Can we con our primitive brain with a false exercise set up and activate other hormones which are normally triggered by endorphin and work out? Imagine your brain reacting as if you have been exercising when in fact you are just sitting in front of the computer. Your mind clears up and you feel fantastic, thanks to the endorphin which makes you happy.

How do you like the sound of them apples? Sounds great, right?

Henriette Van Praag and her team at Purdue University conducted research to test such a set up by injecting lab rats with two medications namely; Aicar and GW1516. These medications had the same structure as substances released from muscles and mixed with blood during real physical exercise. The lab rats responded to the medication instantly, an extraordinary activity was observed in their brains. In the second week of the experiment, better results were achieved in mental tests. Besides, the formation of new neurons in the hippocampus region of their brains accelerated. The researchers thought that they succeeded in deceiving the primitive brain. However, this didn't last long; the brain stopped reacting to the medication in the third week of the experiment. The mental efficiency of the rats dropped below the levels observed for non-exercising ones.[19]

In short, yes, we can deceive our brain to give the same reaction as if we are really exercising but count on the brain sussing out your deception and punishing you for it.

7.

Let's recap: Regular exercise increases mental performance and makes us feel good and happy. It strengthens the memory, protects our health and delays aging on a mid to long term basis.[20] In spite of its great benefits to us, why do people find it difficult to exercise? Why do they start exercise programs with the drive and motivation of Rocky Balboa only to throw in the towel halfway to their goal?

It's because we can't resist the charm of endorphin and find it difficult to go beyond our limits for more and more of it. Yet, the bliss of the moment comes at the expense of fatigue and muscle pain. Whenever we intend to work out again, our primitive brain effectively says, 'well you know what happened the last time, buster!' And reminds us of the price we will pay and therefore we tend to quit. Although we are very well aware of all the benefits of exercising, we just can't get ourselves on the treadmill.

Let's take this one step further.

8.

Spring. Finally, it has stopped raining. The sun shines and makes its existence felt despite the grey clouds that gloomily wander about the sky like depressed cattle over the prairie. The weather is neither hot nor cold. I am walking through the trees in the Belgrade Forest welcomed by joyfully singing birds twittering about the coming of spring. Because it's a week day, there is hardly anyone around.

A sweet breeze from the depths of the forest caresses my face with its invisible hands and the foggy sight of the hills plugs my soul back into the mains. I enjoy being one with nature, I felt free and my mind is at peace. My calf aches but it doesn't really bother me that much as I know it will leave once my muscles warm up. Then, suddenly, I remembered the chain of events which have made me sleepless recently and I go through it scene by scene like a film strip.

My inner voice — not always on my side if truth be told — tells me 'Man up! Put them in their place!' I'm as wound up as the town clock. I take deep breaths as if I am about to go pearl diving and silence the voice and all my negative thoughts. The fresh air in my lungs helps me feel better and my steps get faster as if I am trying to leave all the problems behind. It is like I am trying to get to a place on time. I feel the pressure and the stress leave me with every step I take. I start sweating and the pain in my calf clears to be followed by a feeling of joy. This feeling of intense happiness just lifts me away from my problems. I can feel my soul soar above the, competition, hostility and conceit. My troubles flow away with every single drop of sweat. My body is so light now that surely my feet will leave the ground any minute now. Walking is no longer tiring; I want to walk more and more. Ina few hours I know that pain will set in, yet I can't give it up because of the joy it brings.

To stop walking at this moment will feel like leaving a great table before enjoying the delicious food. I start thinking about why I don't walk more often and find excuses to postpone exercising. Yet, I can't come up with a sound reason. I promise myself that I will come more often. Then, I start pushing my limits and decide to make a few more tours. I enjoy forcing my muscles and can't control this even though I know how it will feel later. Then, on this beautiful spring day, I start running through this fantastic greenery and speed up more and more.

9.

Let's look at this from the joy.ology perspective. The brain starts triggering endorphin the moment he bound out of our front door. Therefore, we don't feel the pain in our muscles. The amount of endorphin grows as we speed happily along. The joy that endorphin brings stimulates us to work harder and harder. Pushing our body limits gives tremendous pleasure so much that marathon runners describe that fantastic moment after hours of running as a 'runner's high'.[21] But, what about later? Once endorphin fades off, the muscle pain comes back (it feels like it comes back to punish you!). The intensity of the pain experienced determines our decision about exercising in the coming days. Due to our primitive brain's sensitivity to negative thoughts, even the thought of exercising is immediately associated with pain and fatigue. We just don't want to make that extra effort. This explains why people usually quit their work out programs in a week. This is why Paul McKenna, who coaches many famous people, from Hollywood celebrities to members of the British Royal family, claims that you should start exercising not in fitness clubs but in every aspect of our lives. Changes such as taking the stairs instead of the lift, walking small distances instead of driving or taking a tour of the neighborhood after getting home.

A great example is the story of Yvonne Meaney who lost 40 kilos and kept it off. Yvonne who had never exercised before in her life started taking her dog for a short walk in the mornings. Then, she increased her tempo gradually and reached a point where she became a marathon runner.[22]

In summary, do you really want to make exercising a part of your life? The golden rule is: Set your limits and do not raise the bar just for the pleasure of it.

The Endorphin Experience

10.

In primitive times, men had to walk for days to hunt. Besides, they didn't have pain killers to ease their suffering when they got wounded (there is currently no evidence of Palaeolithic pharmacies). Then, how did they cope with the muscle pain after these long walks? How did they keep fit and go on with their struggle when they got injured? (Also, no evidence of health clubs or spas back then either). Mankind managed all this, not with aspirin, paracetamol or Ibuprofen plus, but solely with endorphin, passing this magical ability on to future generations through the genes. Today, endorphin functions just the same way; it masks pain. Therefore, as the amount of pain grows, so does the amount of endorphin.[23] I remember an interview with a construction worker who fell from three floors up. He said he felt no pain at the moment of the accident but woke in the hospital in unbearable pain. He had to be given a large amount of really powerful pain killers in the ambulance. Yet the painkillers were not as effective as endorphin.

It is essential to note that endorphin is solely triggered by physical pain.[24] The primitive brain gives priority to the latter even though a broken heart leaves more damage than a broken leg these days. Unfortunately, we don't have a hormone which triggers the pain created by strong emotions. This is why we have to push our bodies physically in order to experience the relief and joy brought on by endorphin.[25] The good news is, that although endorphin is not triggered by emotional pain, it nevertheless takes us away from our problems since it functions as a natural morphine in our body and makes us feel good or even fabulous. In short, we can attain emotional relief by pushing the physical limits of our body. The good thing is, we don't need anyone to trigger endorphin. It is enough to take a walk when we feel bad.[26]

11.

In conclusion, you need to suffer physically in order to trigger endorphin. Since we can't whip ourselves just to inflict the pain exercising stands as the most secure method to trigger endorphin. We don't feel the muscle pain inflicted by exercising, because endorphin won't let us. Besides, the relief brought by endorphin, helps us distance ourselves from our emotional problems and feel happier than a dog with two bones, while increasing our mental performance. Therefore, we can describe endorphin as 'the happiness brought by aches and pains'.

By this definition, we need to stretch our muscles more and more for larger amounts of endorphin or better put, for more happiness. At this point, it is so easy to get caught by endorphin's appeal. But, what then? There are some risks involved:

First of all, post exercise pain can cause us to refrain from it once the effect of endorphin diminishes. That is why in gyms the intensity of exercise programs is gradually scaled up. Even if you were willing to put in loads more effort, a good trainer wouldn't let you.

There are people who can withstand physical pain. Their situation is even worse as they quickly become endorphin addicts. They end up spending most of their time in gyms and face serious health problems as they push their bodies to excessive limits.

Consequently, we will have a life which is more in harmony with our factory settings, when we see endorphin as a tool for relief and protecting our health. This reduces the psychological pressure on us, clears our mind, enhances our memory and lengthens our life. However, there might be grave consequences when endorphin is seen as a source of happiness and we try to substitute for other chemicals.

For each of the hormones covered until now, we underlined their ability to evoke happiness as well as the risks they carry. These hormones which make us happy drift us away to unhappiness at some point. But what if I tell you about a hormone which we can trigger without any limit and has no side effects whatsoever? How would you react to such news?

Thank God, such a hormone actually exists. The fourth hormone which is called OXYTOCIN:

• It can help you overcome problems by transmitting cortisol from our veins.

• It can sustain your well-being by regulating fluctuations in dopamine.

• It can boost your happiness by facilitating the release of serotonin. As a result of all this, we can have a longer, healthier and most importantly of all, a happier life.

It sounds great, right?

That is why we kept the best for last.

PART SEVEN

So glad, I have you

Oxytocin: Trust Fuels Happiness

Dopamine, serotonin and endorphin based happiness is short lived and often brings disappointment. But might there be an alternative? Well there might just be.

Have you ever had that warm fuzzy feeling? You know the one. We feel it after spending quality time with a friend, hugging a loved one, or simply being a positive influence in someone's life. This satisfying response is down to the release of the hardworking hormone; OXYTOCIN. It avoids the highs and lows of dopamine by creating a steady flow of positive fulfilment within the brain. Oxytocin doesn't stop there, though. It plays a key role in releasing stress and in recovering from depression. It is linked with pain relief and healing. It's the reason happy people live longer. In this chapter, you will learn more about this magnificent molecule and discover ways to encourage more oxytocin based happiness.

Roseto Volfortore, a medieval village located 150 kilometers southeast of Rome, on the outskirts of the Apennine Mountains.[1] Life in this village - which looks so cute from outside with its two storey red roofed houses, is not easy at all. The majority of the villagers work in marble quarries in the neighboring hills, while the rest make a living from farming in the valley six kilometers away. They are poor and uneducated; very few of them can read and write.

Towards the end of the nineteenth century, news coming from other end of the ocean becomes a source of hope for the people of Roseto. In 1882, a group of eleven people set sails for New York. After a very hard journey, they spend their first night in a Manhattan bar, sleeping on bar stools. In the beginning, nothing goes right; they don't know what to do or where to live. After a long search, they settled and started working in the slate quarries of Bangor, a town which is 120 kilometers away from Pennsylvania. The following year, fifteen Rosetoeans left Italy to join their fellow men in Pennsylvania. Good stories flowing from the New World accelerated the migration and in mid-1894, almost half of Roseto's population has moved to Pennsylvania. Rosetoeans started buying land on the mountain side near the quarries. They worked and constructed little houses similar to what they had back in Italy. First, they named this new settlement Little Italy, but changed it to Roseto after some years.

In 1896, Pasquale de Nisco, a young and very dynamic priest, began to head the village church. De Nisco initiated the establishment of several associations and organized various festivals in this little town. He encouraged the people to engage in farming in their backyards. While Rosetoeans worked in the slate quarries, they also raise animals and grow many different kinds of fruits and vegetables; from beans to potatoes and grapes. The opening of little shops, bakeries, restaurants and bars follow suit. Soon after, Roseto turned into a self-sufficient town.

Roseto became famous worldwide at the end of 1950's at a seminar organized by a local medical association. After the speech of Steward Wolf, a professor at the University of Oklahoma, one of the local doctors took the floor and said "You know, I've been practicing for seventeen years. I get patients from all over, and I rarely find anyone from Roseto under the age of sixty-five with heart disease." Wolf was taken aback. This was the 1950s, years before the advent of cholesterol-lowering drugs and aggressive measures to prevent heart disease. Heart attacks were an epidemic in the United States. They were the leading cause of death in men under the age of sixty-five. Than, he decided to set up a research into this and a working group was formed with the support of the University of Oklahoma. They examined the family histories, medical records and death certificates of Rosetoeans. Blood samples of almost all residents are collected and electrocardiogram tests carried out.

The results were rather surprising. There was nobody in the town whatsoever that died from a heart attack and not even a symptom of any cardiac disease was observed. Peptic ulcer, a widespread disease at the time, was not seen at all among the people of Roseto. Also cases of suicide, alcoholism and drug addiction were not in existence. According to John Bruhan, a sociologist in Wolf's team, "People of Roseto die of old age. That's it".

Wolf initially assumed that Rosetoeans owe their health to Italian eating habits. However, shortly he discovered that the reason was far different from his assumption, because people of Roseto have actually started cooking with lard instead of olive oil once they moved to America and lipids began to constitute forty-one percent of their calorie intake. For example, their thin pizzas consisting of tomatoes and mozzarella were replaced by really high calorie pizzas covered with lots of salamis and hams. Moreover, Rosetoeans smoked a lot and there was hardly anyone who exercised.

Wolf started to look into genetic factors when he failed to answer the questions from nutrition. He assumed this group of people from the same region of Italy might have originated from a strong and special kind of kin that are immune to the diseases. Fort his, he looked closer into Rosetoeans who lived in different parts of the US. But he found out that they also suffered heart attacks and other diseases just like other people in the States. People of Roseto are no different than an average American once they stepped outside of their town.

Then, he went on to examine the conditions; climate and nature. "Can it be that living on mountain skirts in East Pennsylvania creates a positive impact on health? Or the kind of their daily routine has an invigorating effect? The two closest towns to Roseto were Bangor and Nazareth. These were both about the same size as Roseto, and both were populated with the same kind of hardworking European immigrants. Wolf combed through both towns' medical records. For men over sixty-five, the death rates from heart disease in these towns were three times that of Roseto. Another dead end.

At last, researchers decided to focus on social factors which distinguished Roseto from neighboring towns when nutrition, genetic factors, climate, environment and working conditions were not sufficient to enlighten the mystery of Roseto. In Roseto, unlike the neighboring towns, two or three generations lived in the same house. Besides, people visit each other very frequently and gathered at their backyards to have meals and have fun together. Wolf summarizes his observations in Roseto in his book "The Roseto Story"; "The family ties were really strong unparallel to anywhere else in US. There were twenty two civil society organizations in town even though the population is below two thousand. Cooperation and helping each other was at the peak. The whole town would be mobilized when faced with even the simplest problem. People had trust in one another felt secure."

Wolf and his team had difficulty explaining these results to their colleagues at that time. The suggestion that relations based on trust create magical results on human health was approached with much suspicion by the medical community at an era when developments in genetic and medical technologies were quite popular. Today, thanks to developments in neuroscience we are at the different point.

Friendship and Helping Each Other

1.

To what extent can we generalize the results Wolf obtained from one single town? Are the results still valid till today? Some of these questions might have crossed your mind after you have read Roseto's story and that's why I would like to share the results of two additional research.

In the first study, researchers at Harvard University came up with a questionnaire of two simple questions over a sample of one thousand adults with ages ranging between 34 and 83.[2] The questions are:

• To what extent did you have experienced stress last year?

• How much of your time did you spare for helping your family and friends?

The respondents were monitored for five years. It was observed that the respondents who don't help the people in their surroundings have more than 30% probability of death within five years if faced with problems like financial crisis, loss of a loved one or divorce. No such increase was observed in the death statistics of people who help others.

The results of this research reminded me of the Dead Sea and the Galilee Sea (the biggest water reserve in the country) in Israel.[3] These two lakes actually have same source. However, there was no outlet of water from the Dead Sea and therefore the accumulated salts have destroyed the life in the lake. Yet, life continued in Galilee since the water could easily get out. As a result, contributing and sharing gave life to nature whereas selfishness resulted in death.

In an ongoing study that started in 1940, researchers monitored the private life, work and health conditions of 724 men for seventy-five years.[4] The research sample consisted of two different groups. The first group comprises 2nd grade students in Harvard University and the second group comprises people from the poorest areas of Boston.[5] At the beginning of the study, all respondents were critically interviewed. The interviews were also repeated every two years allowing enough time to monitor their work and private life. They went through series of detailed analysis from blood tests to brain scans. These people grew to be members of different segments of the society. Some became lawyers, some masons, some doctors and one became the president of the United States of America. Some led a happy life and some drifted into alcoholism and drug addiction. A few had been diagnosed with schizophrenia. Sixty percent of the respondents are still alive and continue to be part of the research.[6]

The Role of Mutual Trust for Happier, Healthier and Longer Life

What have seventy-five years of research revealed? What lessons are to be derived from the data that fills thousands of pages? We can group the findings of this research which might be described as "the most extensive research on happiness" under two headings:

First of all, it was found that it wasn't the famous or rich people but rather people with trust based relationships with families and friends who led happier and longer lives with better physical health. Besides, the harms of living alone were revealed. It was observed that the health of people who lived alone deteriorated in their early mid ages, they experienced a reversal in their brain functions, as a result they led a shorter and less happy life.

Secondly, it was understood that people could still be lonely when surrounded by others. In other words, what matters is the quality of the friendships rather than the quantity.

Another finding was how disputes in our life can result into serious health problems. For example, married couples with severe conflicts faced more health problems than singles. Yes, living alone enhances unfavorable outcomes in terms of health and unhappiness but living with somebody and having serious disagreements could be a real disaster.

So, we can summarize the results of these studies as; "Relationships that are based on mutual trust help us to lead a happier, healthier and longer life". It is just that simple.

But then, how do solid and trustful relationships affect our metabolism so that we can have happier, healthier and longer lives? Actually these question is not new; scientists have been searching for answer for decades and almost all experiments and researches point out to one hormone: Oxytocin.[7]

Game of Trust

2.

Let's have a look at a simple experiment designed by Neuro-economist Paul J. Zak in order to understand the chemistry of trust better.[8]

In this experiment called "game of trust", two students were put in different rooms without seeing each other. The student in the first room was given ten US dollars and two options:
• He/She can take the money and leave the room.
• He/She can send all or some of the money to the student in the next room.

If the student picked the second option, the amount of money will be tripled and will be given to the student next room. The student next room has the options to either leave the room with all the money or return some of the money to the student who did the favor. Accordingly, if the first student decides to send $10, the second student will be handed $30 and he will have the options to leave the experiment with all of it or return some of it to the student who has sent the money.

If we evaluate the "game of trust" from the perspective of classical economic theory, the first student could take the ten dollars and leave the experiment with all of the money. If the first student does the unexpected and gives some of the money to the second student then the most logical course of behavior for the second student will be to leave with all the money that was sent to him or her. It makes absolutely no sense to give money to a person you don't know and you will never see.

Zak and his team repeated the "game of trust" with different groups of students for hundreds of times. They collected blood and saliva samples of the students before and after the experiment in order to track the chemical changes in their bodies.

The results were astonishing and surprising. About %90 of the students in the first room sent all or some of the money to the students in the second room. %95 of the students in the second room returned some of the money. But why didn't the students behave logically? What distinguished the students who gave all of the money or some of it from the ones who kept it all?

The results of blood analysis revealed that the key factor that played a role in this decision was a hormone called oxytocin. It seemed that as the amount of oxytocin in the blood increased, the money sent or returned increased as well. The students who took all the money and left the experiment had almost no oxytocin in their blood. When queried about the reason of not sending some of the money to the next door, they unanimously expressed their distrust in students in the next room. So, in short, when there was no oxytocin, there was no trust either. In the absence of trust, people approached each other with suspicion and sharing became impossible.

Having seen these results, you may think the students might have acted under the impact of some other hormones. In order to analyze this, Zak and his team measured nine other molecules that are in interaction with oxytocin. No. Significant increase was observed. This finding showed that there was almost no relation between the feeling of trust and the other molecules.

Besides, the researchers took one step further and considered to artificially increase the amount of oxytocin in the students' bloods. This way they would be able to measure how this hormone influenced behaviors. As it was impossible to penetrate directly to their brains, they gave the students oxytocin via nasal spray. In the group which was given oxytocin from outside, the number of students who sent all their money to the next room doubled immediately. No. Other changes were made in the conditions of the experiment but oxytocin alone had significantly increased the trust for the other.

You may think that all of this was experienced in a laboratory setting and that people would behave differently in the real world. Let's see how the "game of trust" functions outside a lab in order to clarify the questions on your mind.

3.

George checked the time, it was a hectic day. He still had two hours and twenty-three minutes to the end of the day; time was not passing. His life was boring whereas he started working in the gas station only last week. Being a cashier wasn't worthy of him. He felt as he was a university graduate with a degree in economics. He deserved better but just couldn't get a job he wanted despite all his efforts.

A well groomed man walked in as George was immersed deep in his thoughts. You could read the anxiety and panic from his face. He was carrying a flamboyant box; he approached George and asked politely;

"I have a job interview in an hour. I don't know what to do with it, will you please help me?"

George couldn't make anything of what he said. "How can I help you?" he asked.

The man opened the box and showed a necklace. "I just found this box on the sink in the men's room. It is a beautiful piece. Has anyone come looking for this?"

"No, no one has come yet."

"Will you please have a closer look? It is a very valuable piece; the person who lost it must be devastated now. What do you think we should do? How can we reach its owner?"

George examined the necklace; it really looked dazzling under the light. At the moment, the phone started ringing. George answered; a man in panic was on the line "I used your station's toilet about ten minutes ago and I forgot the necklace I bought for my wife."

"Calm down" George said. "The fellow who found it is here now with the necklace."

"I can't believe it. I don't know how to thank you; I am really grateful. There is a bit of traffic but I will be there in half an hour at most. Please tell that very gracious man that I would like to offer him $500 to express my gratitude".

The man who found the necklace didn't seem to be very much impressed and happy about the prize.

"No, I can't wait any more; I have already lost a lot of time. I don't want to be late for my interview. Is there anything we can do about this?"

"I will be here for another two hours; I can hand in the necklace to him on your behalf."

"Can you really do that?" he asked. He heaved a sigh of relief and said "That will be just great, then let's share this reward."

"Really?" asked George in amazement as he had to work for almost fifteen days to make that $250.

"Certainly" said the man and started looking worried again. "I have no idea at what time my interview will finish and I live quite far from here" he said.

"No problem" George said and gave him $250 from the cash register. George smiled and said "Let me give your share in advance and I will put it back once the goofy husband comes and gives the $500."

The guy left the market in a hurry, almost running. George first thought he was hurrying to his interview realized that he was fooled when two hours passed without anyone showing up to pick the necklace. He was left with nothing but an imitation necklace in his hands.

How could he be so stupid? How could he be duped so easily? Why did he trust a guy he didn't know?

Let's go back to the "game of trust" in order to answer these questions. Remember that the people in the game didn't know each other as well. However, one person putting trust in the other triggered large amounts of oxytocin which in turns created trust on the other side as well. We experience the same thing in real life; when we feel we are relied upon, we start feeling trust in that person as well. This is how our primitive brain functions.

Crooks fool us by playing on this precious part of our brain. Remember that George didn't know the guy and normally shouldn't have trusted him. However, when he trusted and handed the necklace, George felt assured. Besides, the guy made a great gesture by offering to share the reward with him. George, very much under the impact of large amount of oxytocin released, reacted immediately in order to return the favor that was extended to him. And you know the rest.

4.

Robert B. Cialdini, in his book "Psychology of Persuasion", named this state of mind as "the rule of reciprocation".[9] According to Cialdini, we become suddenly defenseless when someone do us a favor. The favor evokes trust for the other; trust eliminates suspicion and we tend to obey automatically and say "yes" to the requests of people whom we rely upon. This principle is not only utilized by crooks but also by advertisers, our colleagues, and friends and even by people we are romantically involved with. We are basically the victims of our brain's vulnerability in this regard. Therefore, we need to understand which point things get out of control so that we don't get caught in the trap of trust.

5.

Mary retired from a public bank eight years ago. After her retirement, she became active in several civil organizations and started working in the women's branch of the political party she has been supporting and voted in favor for years. She took great pride and pleasure in doing voluntary work and contributing to the society. She found herself in a period of hustle and bustle during the campaign for the local elections but she had no complaints. However, she was worried about getting similar results with the previous general election. Four years ago, they could hardly reach %15 in spite of all the hard work they put in the campaign. Now, in order for their candidate to be elected, %40 of the votes are a requirement. This was not easy at all.

Being aware of the situation, their candidate asked them to move with a different strategy. During this campaign;

• They would donate box containing victuals to families.

• Only families physically present will be given the boxes as no collection by proxy is accepted.

• The visit will only be strictly for listening to wishes, yearnings and complaints of the people and not some sort of political jamboree or propaganda.

These rules which Mary couldn't make any sense of were also unwelcomed by other members of the women's branches. Many of them believed that it is not only wrong to try buying votes in return to victuals but also useless. Besides, if it weren't for the party propaganda, what was the point of paying home visits? During heated conversations about the matter, Belgin, one of the members, came forward and said "I am not going to follow these ridiculous rules and I will withdraw my support if they insist on them." Belgin's views mattered since she was a member of the party for a very long time. Some of the women supported her while some other remained silent.

Mary didn't like to stretch the rules maybe because of her long years of service in public sector. That is why she delivered every single thing that was expected of her. She visited an average of eight or ten families every day. She listened to their problems with patience and took notes. On the day of the election, she was in charge of the ballot box of the region which she was responsible for. She welcomed all the families she visited earlier with a warm smile, shook hands and after voting sent them off by wishing "Let us hope for the best for all of us." She was really curious about the election results. "I wish I could have made a bit of propaganda; explain the party agenda and plans" she was saying to herself.

In the evening, when the ballot boxes were opened she had mixed feelings; both sorrow and joy at the same time. Her party could only reach 28% but in her box a record of forty-seven percent was achieved. It was unbelievable; she had difficulty in explaining this situation. However, she was able to draw some conclusions when she reviewed the entire process in detail;

• It is more effective to listen people instead of trying to be an impostor.

• Nothing can substitute for the trust created by caring and sincerity.

• The presentation of gift matter more than the gift itself.

Most important of all, she understood why they failed in every election.

6.

What would you think about giving people money instead of distributing victuals before the elections? Logically reasoning, this tells us that giving money makes more sense since this would enable them to buy what they really need instead of the things you supply them. Yet, this option is not put into consideration since our primitive brain is not familiar with the concept of money. Money makes people happy but only for a short time; however, presents carry meanings beyond their values.[10]

What would you think if a friend tells you that he donated $1000 for the Education Volunteers Foundation? Probably the question "Why is he telling people that he made a donation?" will cross your mind. Now suppose the same person told you that he volunteered to paint the school in her neighborhood to support the same foundation. How would you react to that? Yes, you respect him more. You may even suggest that you two may work together in the following week when in fact the commercial value of painting walls is not above $50.

It is a similar case with the parenting styles. Some parents help their children with their studies, cook for them and go shopping together while some others give only money for these chores to be taken care of. Which parenting style would you think makes the kids respect their parents more?

If this hasn't convinced you yet, then imagine this scenario. A couple gets together for dinner. The guy proposes her but can't give her a ring and instead gives her money to buy herself the ring she wishes. Probably this would cause quite an 'emotional outburst'.

Against all these examples you might still say "I prefer money" since it gives us the freedom to pursue/purchase our wish; increases our options. However, since they are actualized on a rational level, they won't make a lasting impact. They can't activate emotions such as commitment or loyalty whereas a small gift evokes an emotional impact that triggers oxytocin which in turn creates mutual trust and strengthens bonds between people. As far as it existed, a gift would remind of the person and the moment it was given. The trust for the other is refreshed every time that pleasant memory is envisaged in mind.

7.

How does the chemistry of trust function in family relations, work life and other social interactions? How can we establish satisfying and long lasting relationships? How can we create the ideal family and the ideal work place? Let's answer this with a real life example.

It is quite popular e-commerce company. Let us name it allsale.com. The owners set out to establish an ideal company and work with several consultants to this end; the latest technology, advanced software, up-to-date management approach, modern systems etc. They put together everything necessary for "success". They also paid special attention to their work environment; cafes, game rooms, gym and even a swimming pool. This magnificent office became headlines in newspapers and business magazines and everyone was fascinated when they enter the premises.

Yet, something seems to be wrong despite all the efforts and investments; they fail to satisfy the employees and this reflects on the performance directly. The company faces absenteeism, turn over and tardiness rates that are above the sector average. To crown it all, it was observed that some employees damaged the company deliberately; they put out cigarettes on game consoles and tear the leather sofas. The company owners have difficulty in understanding this kind of attitude and changed the CEO and the human resources director as a resort.

The new management examines the results of earlier surveys and conducted one-one interviews with the employees in order to identify the source of employee dissatisfaction. When all data were aggregated and analyzed, they found out that the employees don't feel safe and the level of trust upon the management is low yet the reasons of distrust remain unknown. The human resources director began to review all the factors he thinks might influence trust. For instance; checking the payment dates of salaries but spotted no delays. There was no one wrongfully terminated or any case of unpaid indemnity. The employees don't mention any specific reason either. They just pointed out to a partially paid bonus. When examined, it turned out that the management promised two months' salaries worth of bonus in case of profit. However, things didn't go well and they closed the year with a record loss. Yet, still, the employees were given one salary bonus.

I met with the human resources director of the company at a "Chemistry of Happiness" seminar where he gave a detailed account of the whole process and asked my opinion. I redirected the question to him and asked about his own views regarding the reason for the employees distrust.

"I was thinking that our employees were spoiled rotten before I listened to your speech" he said.

"And what do you think now?"

"Well, unfortunately we don't trust them. We monitor everything they do with cameras; we check their entrance and exits with finger print tracking and check all their activities on the net through IT reports. We don't let them even breathe without our knowledge."

"But why do you do all this?"

"In order to ensure high performance."

"And do you get high performance from them?"

"No, and that is our problem actually."

"What next?"

"I suppose we need to look at this matter from a different perspective."

After this short conversation, the owners gathered all the employees to announce that the company is entering a new phase. They informed that the company will be functioning on a more corporate basis built on the principle of trust. This was followed by a considerable amount of cut down in all the control mechanisms and monitoring systems at allsale.com. Cameras, computer monitoring systems and finger print sensors were removed. Section managers were given more initiative. None of these changes were simple and the new management was in fact taking a great risk. However, the outcome was amazing. Employee performance exceeded expectations instantly. Record improvements were observed in surveys which were carried out by independent research companies to measure trust and employee satisfaction. The company has become one of the best employers in the country and this was made possible without spending a penny; merely by letting the employees aware that they are entrusted by the management.

How would you feel when a person doesn't trust you and makes it obvious with his or her attitude and behavior? In other words, would you be able to rely on somebody who doesn't trust you? Our logic tells us that keeping promises is sufficient for creating trust however trust is a mutual feeling;[11] being a man of his word is necessary but doesn't suffice alone to evoke the feeling of trust. Therefore, if we wish to gain the trust of our spouse, children, friends and employees, we need to take the initial step ourselves and first let them feel entrusted.

Physical Contact

8.

Have you ever heard of such news as this? "Last night, there was a plane crash, six people who managed to hold hands survived while 173 people couldn't make it". The question is "Why we immediately hold our spouse's or children's hands when we enter an air pocket?" Now imagine the moment, when a child finds his parents after getting lost in a shopping mall. Probably, the mother would embrace and hold her child tightly when he or she runs to her. In fact, there is no logical explanation to this behavior either, why does the kid nestle in the mother, who is the kid afraid of? Or, who is she protecting her child from?

Why do people feel the need to hold hands or embrace each other like the ones above? That is because physical contact increases the amount of oxytocin produced by our brain. Embracing and holding hands won't save us from unpleasant situation; however, it will provide some relief, thanks to the extra oxytocin it renders. This is why a lost child holds his mother tightly to feel safe again or we wish to hold somebody's hands when the plane gets into turbulence. Similarly, a crying baby is soothed when he or she is held by the mother; it is oxytocin in action created by physical contact.[12]

Now, imagine yourself signing an important contract; this might be for starting a partnership. The signatures are complete and you stepped forward to shake your new partner's hand. What if your new partner doesn't respond? How would you feel if he tells his signature is enough and he believes it is a "stupid" ritual to shake hands? Not so good I think. Basically, physical contact triggers the release of oxytocin which works towards fulfilling the need of trust evoked by this new contract. This is why in many cases; hand shaking is followed by kissing on the cheek and sometimes holding and embracing.

9.

In the last decade, we have witnessed extra ordinary developments in the field of medicine; many diseases implicated to be problems within this period. Great progress has been achieved in the treatment of cancer, thanks to smart medication. Advances in imaging technologies have increased the accuracy of diagnosis; the era of bloodless surgery has begun; transplant is now possible almost for all organs. These developments have improved the quality of life and life expectation.

What about trusting the doctors? So can't we assume that the patients trust the doctors more now because they make more accurate diagnosis, apply extensive treatments and perform better operations? Unfortunately, the answer is NO! Statistics revealed that in the last decade trust for doctors has dropped significantly. According to a study by Robert Blendon and his team which was published in the New England Journal of Medicine, every patient out of two doesn't trust his or her doctor.[13] Why this?

Abraham Verghese, professor of medicine at Stanford University said that we entered a phase in medicine in which technology has replaced physical examination.[14] The doctors review data on computers instead of the patients themselves. This approach saves time and brings about more accurate diagnosis yet the patients can't feel this. They expect to be physically examined and told about what is going on. This lack of attention causes reduced trust for the doctor and also weakens the faith in the treatment given.

You might think that Verghese's ideas are quite assertive. You may find it difficult to relate an old fashioned method of treatment with the feeling of trust. To address such concerns we have we have presented a small survey of two questions on the internal medical service of hospitals to a total of 400 patients:

1. Do you have trust in the treatment prescribed by your doctor?

2. Did your doctor examine you physically?

63% of the patients responded positively to the first question for whom the doctors who didn't make a physical examination. This rate jumped to 94%, for doctors who actually made a physical examination. The traditional patient-doctor contact boosted the trust in the doctors by 31%.

These results indicated an obvious discrepancy between the doctors' and the patients' notion of "good medical service". Doctors are more interested in the efficiency and activity aspect of the practice while the patients wish to receive the message "You matter most and I will do the best I can for you" which can be conveyed via physical examination that makes the release of oxytocin possible. Abraham Verghese supported this view by claiming that "The biggest breakthrough in medicine to come in the next 10 years would be the rediscovery of human hand - to touch, to comfort, to diagnose and to bring about treatment".[15]

10.

In our day, it is not only the field of medicine that we experience loss of trust. There is a serious eroding of confidence within families, friendships and work environment which results in increasing numbers of divorces and unemployment. Many people complained about the nature of modern friendships and yearn for the old ones; we all long for having people around us whom we can really rely on.

But how much time do we spare for our loved ones? How close are we to them? How many times in a day do we hold, embrace, kiss and joke with them? We spend most of our time in front of the computer, TV or with our phones. People prefer to send messages instead of talking to each other. The virtual world has become more essential than the real one. Every day, we move away from our factory settings more and more. And it is no good for our happiness.

11.

Oxytocin against dopamine and serotonin… If you were to make a choice, which one would you prefer? Is it a difficult decision to make? Let's make it more concrete. If I give you an envelope with $20 in it and tell you that;
• You may spend it for yourself or
• You might use it to do good for someone else.

Which option would you think would make you happier and pick?

Researchers at the University of British Colombia, Canada conducted a similar experiment on students where some of the students were given the liberty to spend the money as they pleased and the rest were asked to use it for other people.[16] The students in the first group felt luckier in the beginning and the ones in the second group concealed their unhappiness about this. At the end of the day, the students were asked how they spent the money and how they felt. The students in the first group purchased things like t-shirts, cosmetics, ear rings etc. The students in the second group bought things for their loved ones or made donations to civil organizations. For the students who spent the money for themselves, the joy of buying had ceased already and they weren't feeling anything. However, in the second group- the good doers, the joy still lasted. Later, the study was repeated in an entirely different culture in Uganda. The results were the same.

Another example. Gallup, the biggest research company of the world, in the "Happiness Survey" which covered 136 countries, asked two questions:

1. Have you donated any money to a charity organization lately?
2. How happy are you in life, generally?

The study revealed that people who donated were significantly happier in all these countries.[17]

Let's go back to our question, oxytocin against dopamine and serotonin... Which one? Dopamine and serotonin can produce happiness but only momentarily. However, it is only with oxytocin that we can attain permanent and sustainable joy.[18]

12.

As you may remember, endorphin enables us to feel better by reducing the adverse effects of cortisol. In fact, in our brain oxytocin functions in a similar method but it is more powerful than endorphin and provides a longer lasting effect.[19]

Imagine you work in competitive company and wish to replace the marketing director who will retire soon. You believe that you deserve the position and show tremendous effort to earn it. Then, it the end of the year, the promotions were announced. Just as you are waiting for the good news, you found out that you were fired.

Let's evaluate the rest from the joy.ology perspective. Dopamine and serotonin that are triggered by the hope of getting promoted are replaced by cortisol the moment you get the bad news. Your brain gets alarmed and pressures you to do something about it. You feel awful; you need to get rid of the cortisol in your blood. You start searching for ways to trigger the happy chemicals. There is no chance of triggering dopamine or serotonin by natural methods since there is no possibility of a promotion or a new job at that very moment. You are aware that shortcuts such as alcohol or drugs will harm you and will make things even worse in the long run. You just want to get out; in a few minutes you find yourself walking, taking fast steps, in the park across the office. This helps to release endorphin which gives you a bit of comfort, yet, it is not sufficient. Then you begin to search for another solution. First, you call your wife and then friends. Talking to them gets off some of the pressure but the real relief comes when you see them waiting at your door. You embrace your loved ones immediately and start feeling much better; to an extent you can't make sense of it. This is due to the large amount of oxytocin triggered by physical contact.

13.

You must have heard of Alcoholics Anonymous.[20] They define themselves as "a fellowship of men and women who share their experience, strength and hope with each other that they may solve their common problem and help others to recover from alcoholism". They operate in 178 countries. They don't work with psychiatrists or psychologists; don't offer professional therapy but nevertheless, helped hundred thousands of alcoholics to get their lives back. How do they manage this? Actually, it is quite simple. They bring together the alcoholics who hope to recover and drive them to help one another. That's it.

If we look at the processes for the joy.ology perspective, oxytocin that is triggered by these meetings makes them feel good about themselves and provide a sense of security. They understand that they are not alone and desperate. They exchange experiences with members, make suggestions and support each other at times of difficulty. This is how they enjoy supporting and making a difference in other people's lives. In short, the life styles of Alcoholics Anonymous members change in a way to accommodate higher oxytocin release. Kindness and solidarity revokes joy to replace the virtual world which is created by dopamine with the consumption of alcohol.

14.

The US soldiers were fighting in extremely hard conditions in Vietnam where drugs were in extremely within reach. According to Times magazine, using heroine became almost as common as chewing gums among US soldiers. It was believed at least 20% of the army became drug addicts. The American society feared that junkies who are Vietnam veterans would fill up the streets after the war. Then, the war was over and the soldiers went back home. What do you think happened? Ninety five percent of the addicts stopped using drugs within a year without any medical support. As for the remaining 5%, not much progress was achieved despite all the therapy and medical treatment. The situation was hard to explain.

Professor Bruce K. Alexander and his team at Simon Fraser University closely examined both groups to explain the present situation. They tried to identify the factors which make it easy to break drug addiction. Findings showed that the ones who had family and friend support after the war could easily give up drugs, whereas the soldiers who were unemployed and on their own weren't able to break the addiction irrespective of all medical support.[21]

Another research which was conducted in the University of Northern Carolina in 2012, revealed that in the United States, the majority of alcohol and heroine survivors got support from their families and friends and that the amount of oxytocin in their blood is much higher than the other addicts.[22]

From now on, if somebody tells you "I wouldn't be able to overcome the hardships without the support of my family and friends", you can translate this into "If I didn't find the way to trigger oxytocin, I wouldn't be able to discharge the large amount of cortisol in my blood".

15.

We have emphasized that oxytocin has a key role in breaking alcohol or drug addictions.[23] What about the initial stages of such habits? Can it have a preventive effect?

It is a known fact that lonely people are more likely to get addicted to drugs. However, with this data, it would be over-emphasizibg that that oxytocin can help prevent addiction. Therefore, let's review the "Addiction Experiment" designed by Professor Bruce K. Alexander before reaching a conclusion.[24]

Professor Bruce K. Alexander, at the initial phase of the experiment, left food and two bowls of water in a cage where there is only one rat inside. One of the bowls contains regular water while the other contains water with morphine. Although, the rat showed no interest in the beginning but sooner it starts to show a special liking to the water with morphine mix which later turned into an addiction. Professor Bruce K. Alexander repeats the experiment with different rats but gets the same result every time. Then he increased the number of rats and puts simple toys for entertainment. In his own words, he turned the cage into a rat park. The rats tried the water with morphine but don't go near it again; not even a single rat gets attracted by it.

This experiment indicated that drug usage is in fact the brain's ambient host for happiness. In cases where happy chemicals are deficient, the primitive brain tries to fill this void with short-cuts like alcohol and drugs. Yet, this makes things worse and upsets the entire balance. No pursuit is called for when the happy chemicals are triggered within balance. In this respect, oxytocin is extremely critical in keeping this balance.

16.

A healthy, happy and long life is what we all wish for. Thank God, now, we have detailed knowledge about the key chemical which is needed for this: Oxytocin. This magnificent molecule goes beyond making us feel good; it helps us to overcome our problems fast without damage.[25] Besides, oxytocin is triggered quite easily. It is enough to be with our loved ones and feel the mutual trust. That is to say, unlike dopamine or serotonin, we don't have to work day and night and stri-ve for others' admiration.

Then, why has trust become one of the most basic problems in our day? In short, why have triggering oxytocin become so difficult?

In fact, the answer lies within this statement we lose our potential of triggering oxytocin when trapped in the appeal of dopamine and serotonin. To be more precise, huge goals and daily routines eats into our time with so that we have little or no time to spend with our loved ones, our colleagues have become our rivals because of the changed rules of the business life and status struggle damages our friendships and virtual relationships weaken real ones. As a result, families are destroyed and relationships that are based on self-interests replace true friendships. People become prisoners of money, ambition and status struggle or in other words, become enslaved by the chains of dopamine and serotonin so they end up leading a lonely life within crowds.

If we wish to attain an acme of sustainable happiness, we have to stop neglecting our families and friends and spare time for them, that way we are at full potential of triggering oxytocin.

PART EIGHT

The Joy.ology Model

Chain Reaction: Wonderful Life

Wonderful life: Everybody's shared dream. Now we know more about the hormones which can make this possible how we can bring about such a change. In summary, mankind needs to accomplish thing to feel happy. Success is the prerequisite of happiness. Yet, how we achieve success matters more than anything else. If we set out to the journey of success on our own, we become addicted to one single chemical, dopamine. We find it difficult to trigger serotonin when others ignore our achievements. Lack of trust consumes us. We can't find happiness even though we have "everything". Then, what is the solution? The solution is pretty clear. Setting out to the journey of success with others and enjoying the ride instead of only focusing on results. Now, let's see how we can make these come alive by going through real life examples.

Throughout this book, we have seen how our brains chemically create happiness with shallow disregard for our opinions on the matter. When confronted with an existential threat our brains sound the alarm by activating the hormone cortisol. We experience this alarm as anxiety, stress and fear. The negative feelings we have when hungry, when sitting in heavy traffic, when criticized by others or when faced with a dangerous animal — all stem from cortisol. The brain is fairly magnanimous in this regard and rewards our best efforts with a blast of another substance in its chemical arsenal: dopamine. We are relieved, grateful even. We feel good and happy. Therefore, while cortisol helps us withdraw from life's less enjoyable moments dopamine gets right in their and points out what needs to be done for a better life, then sets us in motion.

If what we do is recognised and appreciated by others, our brain triggers a third hormone called serotonin, boosting our happiness once more. When we choose to work for the common good and contribute to the well-being of others rather than pander to our own self interest, a fourth hormone named oxytocin kicks in. And takes us to an entirely different dimension. Confidence generated by oxytocin strengthens our resistance to challenge. In short, even though we are always rewarded for overcoming challenges on our own, the grand award comes if we function with the people around us and when our resolutions are accepted by them as well.

And of course, there is the dimension of physical endurance. In response to hard physical effort, the brain deploys another hormone: endorphin. This attenuates muscle pain and endorphin allows us to continue our activities without performance loss. Although the primary function of endorphin is to mask physical pain, it also counters the effects of cortisol. That's why at times of stress, leaping about a gymnasium in our Lycra leggings helps us feel good.

1.

By now you should have a thorough understanding of the contribution of each hormone in creating happiness, their short and long term effects and how they are triggered. Let's summarize all this knowledge in the "Happiness Matrix".

Individual Performance	High	3- Narcissist, Fragile, Insecure 'Only I know what is best and can do it' 'I am important and I don't need anyone.' Output: Loneliness Source of Happiness: Dopamine	4- Happy, Peaceful 'I am aware of my shortcomings.' 'We can combine our strengths to create a synergy.' Output: Chain Reaction Source of Happiness: Dopamine, Serotonin, Oxytocin
	Low	1-- Inconsiderate, Lazy, Selfish 'Hard work and effort won't take me anywhere.' 'I don't help people. Kindness won't bring any good.' 'I have to find someone to blame when things go wrong.' Output: Despair Source of Happiness : Nothing	2- Meek, Unqualified 'I need others to stand on my feet.' 'I can't do anything on my own.' Output: Meekness, Needy Source of Happiness: Oxytocin
		Low	High
		Cooperation	

Happiness Matrix

Remember how the brain uses happiness to rewards our efforts to survive and passes our genes on to the next generation. Different awards await us depending on whether these efforts are made

alone or in collaboration with others. Based on this, we can conclude that '*Individual Performance*' and '*Cooperation*' are the two basic factors that determine how happy we are.

Here, individual effort translates to the following statement: 'Only I know what's best and I can do it. I don't need anyone else.' The cooperative approach on the other hand is epitomised by the statement, 'Sustainable success is possible only with the help and support of others'. People can choose whether to work singly or with others, which ever suits them best therefore, based on our preferences, we are placed in any of the quadrants above.

3- Narcissist, Fragile, Insecure	*4- Happy, Peaceful*
1- Inconsiderate, Lazy, Selfish 'Hard work and effort won't take me anywhere.' 'I don't help people. Kindness won't bring any good.' 'I have to find someone to blame when things go wrong.' Output: *Despair* Source of Happiness: *Nothing*	*2- Meek, Unqualified*

Those in the first region of the matrix are classified '*inconsiderate*'. When seeking to achieve something, such people eschew individual effort but simultaneously avoid cooperation with others too. They don't have any significant success in life. They spend their time complaining and feeling sorry for themselves. They hold others responsible — parents, friends, teachers and even the stars for what they experience in life. They are extremely defenseless against shortcuts to happiness such as alcohol and drugs since they aren't able to trigger happy chemicals in natural ways. In other words, you may strike these people off your Christmas card list, there's nothing to be gained having a relationship with them.

3- Narcissist, Fragile, Insecure	4- Happy, Peaceful
1- Inconsiderate, Lazy, Selfish	2- Meek, Unqualified 'I need others to stand on my feet.' 'I can't do anything on my own.' Output: *Meekness, Needy* Source of Happiness: *Oxytocin*

Square two of the matrix is reserved for people who believe they can achieve what they want only with the help of others. These are classified '*meek*'. The bible claimed that the meek would inherit the earth, but they have low self confidence and can't decide on their own or take action, so what good the earth is going to do them, heaven knows. They can have a sense of security by becoming part of a group or community and following their leaders unconditionally. If you are the kind of person who would wear your underpants on your head if a charismatic figure commanded you to, you might belong in this group. Basically, they could not find their butt using both hands and for this reason should also be struck of your Christmas card list. Their source of happiness is limited merely to oxytocin due to their incapacity to accomplish things on their own. The absence of achievement in their lives which consolidates their lack of recognition. This in turn evokes a feeling of lowliness which they can't get over.

3- Narcissist, Fragile, Insecure	4- Happy, Peaceful
'Only I know what is best and can do it' 'I am important and I don't need anyone.' Output: *Loneliness* Source of Happiness: *Dopamine*	
1- Inconsiderate, Lazy, Selfish	2- Meek, Unqualified

The third square enshrines the rising values of the twenty first century: freedom, liberation from chains, proving one's own self and going one's own way. We are literally in a period when individual success is glorified — sanctified even. Grading systems at schools and performance appraisals in the work place fuel individual success. Popular media continuously present recipes for individual success, completely overlooking cooperation, communication and teamwork. From scientists to entrepreneurs, actors, singers and football players, people who become prominent through individual success boost the popularity of the third square. However, most of the people can't see the fact that this inclination condemns them to only one single source of happy chemical, namely dopamine. Although they are individually powerful they fail to find the people who will applaud their achievements and support them in times of need. This situation blocks the release of serotonin and oxytocin, creating feelings of loneliness and insecurity. They try to cover this happiness deficit with more and more dopamine. This raises the bar of success or in joy.ology terms, results in the raising of the dopamine threshold day by day. They can't find joy in small things and life loses its color. In short, through time, the lifestyle they always desired and worked for becomes their biggest dead end.

3- Narcissist, Fragile, Insecure	4- Happy, Peaceful
	'I am aware of my shortcomings.' 'We can combine our strengths to create a synergy.' Output: *Chain Reaction* Source of Happiness: *Dopamine, Serotonin, Oxytocin*
1- Inconsiderate, Lazy, Selfish	2- Meek, Unqualified

The focus of the fourth square is the creation of shared values. In this square, the interests of others have as much value as our own. Success is collectively owned. Difficulties are confronted together. However, this lifestyle doesn't allow us to go our own way or act as we please. To use a relationship analogy, you can move in with your long-term partner but you can't have the TV remote all to yourself. On the face of it, giving up some personal freedom to pursue the approval of others lacks appeal. Unfortunately, we have no alternative for inducing a chain reaction except by activating all happy chemicals at the same time.

As unreasonable as it seems, our primitive brain, in charge of governing the happy chemicals functions in this way. For instance, think of the moments when your immediate environment ignores your accomplishments. The happiness which used dopamine as a springboard is not complete. Similarly, fat bank accounts won't give you the pleasure derived from the warmth and trust provided by friends.

To conclude, happy chemicals are not designed to work independently of each other; they closely interact; they're like old pals. The fourth Square is the only region where these interactions function healthily, triggering happy chemicals at the highest level. We end up on other squares when the chemical balance and interactions in our brain are damaged, making it hard to reach sustainable happiness.

Let's now go through our individual journey of happiness.

Journey of Happiness

2.

We descend to earth in the second square, babies totally dependent on others. To survive, we need someone to feed us, put us to sleep, take us to the doctor when we're sick. In short, we need to be completely taken care of. Taking care of these demands isn't easy for our parents, but thanks to oxytocin they take great pleasure taking care of us. Besides, oxytocin enhances a solidification of mutual trust and affection, it makes us a family. Many people marry and have children so as to amass enough joy that oxytocin can provide them with.

Our struggle for independence starts the moment we are born. Our desire is to escape the Second Square and move into the Third.

At first, achievements such as learning to speak, crawl and walk fill us with hope. Everything we do is applauded by our family and this triggers the release of serotonin which evokes feelings of superiority.

We begin to think that we have the power to dominate and get everything we want. The bubble bursts when other kids get involved. The happy chemicals supplied unconditionally by our parents in our inner world cannot be found in the outer world. Even though we can't name them, we discover that dopamine comes from success; serotonin from appreciation and oxytocin from establishing strong friendships. That's how our battle to move to the fourth square kicks off. Showing others how important we are and proving ourselves becomes our priority. We strive to trigger these three chemicals. Some add endorphin to their happiness cocktail, with sport become an integral part of their life. These types can often be found running up mountains white water kayaking. If, over time, we establish relationships based on trust we may manage to transfer ourselves to the fourth square. We can easily activate the happy chemicals because the contributions and support of others help us achieve success earlier. Besides, we will have people around us to appreciate our accomplishments and their presence gives us a feeling of security in hard times.

Those who fail to gain such support over time may give up their efforts to establish meaningful relationships and end up back in the third square. Achieving success and feeling superior to others becomes their top priority and purpose in life. They are often surrounded by false friends (the worst kind). In successful times, they cannot find anyone to congratulate them with sincerity.

They accuse those around them of jealousy. Their bitter feelings prevent them from enjoying the pride and joy for their achievements. They hide their fragility and craving for love behind a mask. Some hide their true feelings with fake smiles to present a rosy picture to others. Yet, nothing they do can substitute for the serotonin and oxytocin gap; they can't find true happiness. In short, the people in this Square might be gloriously successful but not as happy in the true sense.

What about those who fail to make any personal achievements — the people in the Third Square? They have two choices. Those who choose to obey, go back to the Second Square. They win the love of people whom they see as their protector and leader by pampering them. Gaining the support of powerful people gives them a sense of security. However, failing to accomplish something on their own eats them up and leaves them with a feeling of lowliness. They may lead a peaceful but unhappy life.

People who refuse to obey despite their personal failure reach deadlock. They don't stand a chance of triggering happy chemicals naturally. They live on the edge of emotional bankruptcy. They try to close the gap created by the absence of happy chemicals in their lives by choosing dopamine shortcuts such as nicotine, tequila and breaking the speed pizza-eating world record. Drug addiction is pretty common among people in this Square. We might observe that those unsuccessful and unsupported are easily bogged down in alcoholism or drug abuse.

Four Rooms

3.

The Joy.ology model reminds me of the Quentin Tarantino movie 'Four Rooms'. Four rooms in a luxurious but out of favor hotel. Four interesting lives. Our hero, Ted who starts working as a service man in the New Year's eve, witnessed different situations in every room he knocked. Now, let us take a similar tour in the rooms of the joy.ology model. I would like you to compare the story in every room to your own life and decide which conveys a message.

Room No 1: Tom

Tom forced himself out from under the bedcovers like the Creature from the Black Lagoon, having battered the snooze button on his alarm hard enough to break it. He'd spent the whole night systematically drinking his way through the bar's stock of single malt whiskies in alphabetical order. He couldn't even remember at what time he'd returned to his room. He did remember the painful memory of trying for an hour the take his trousers off over his head. It was well after sun up but the thick hotel curtains almost totally prevented sunlight entering the room.

The room was almost pitch dark. He groped for the cigarette pack. His mind was so blurred that he didn't notice that he'd lit the cigarette on the wrong side until the first puff. The cigarette burst into flames and he tumbled down the bed while desperately trying to put out. Then, he burst into tears. He was in Chicago for an important sales meeting but had no energy at all, not even to move an inch. How did this happen?

Tom was 48 years old. He didn't like being called lazy but hated working. Loafing around, achieving results through short cuts and gaining favor by using other people became his motto for life. His friends back in high school used to joke that he could be top of the class if he just used the time he spent cheating to study instead (He had developed his own personal methods of cheating). He would say 'I can't give up my principles'. He'd join projects groups with the most hardworking students and get good grades without personal effort. This was how he managed to get certificates of excellence throughout his high school years and make his family proud.

However, a few chickens came home to roost at university exam time. First two years, he failed to enroll in a university. On his third attempt, with difficulty and with no scholarship he managed to secure a place at Cameron University, Faculty of Office Management. His family was not wealthy but his parents were ready make sacrifices so they could see Tom graduate. Tom had no idea what Office Management meant when he started college, and still didn't the day of his graduation. He found work a couple of times but neither occasion led to a positive outcome. He believed he was born to be a manager, not for trivial work. He didn't have the discipline regular office life demanded. He wanted an easy life with more flexible hours, so he decided he would become a sales representative. He just hung around all day with his company car. In his 23 years of professional life, Tom changed job 16 times. In almost every new job, he instantly became popular but he just as quickly fell out of favor. He was unemployed at times but his wife never made an issue over it; she had a steady job as a nurse. They'd been classmates in high school and his marriage was his only achievement in life.

Unlike Tom, she was hard working and disciplined. Overtime at the hospital, night shifts and housework kept her extremely busy. She was very polite and sensitive; afraid to upset him she never complained about Tom's situation. And, what about Tom? He cheated on his wife several times. Mary suspected at times but Tom somehow managed to get away with it — until he had an affair with the house maid. The woman blackmailed him for some time but then told Mary everything. They promptly divorced. Mary didn't ask for alimony. Tom could hardly make ends meet as it was. Tom became a real mess after the divorce. He was about to be fired from the company he'd worked for for the last 2 years. Luckily, his boss was an understanding man who had also gone through a divorce. He wanted to help Tom even though there wasn't much he could do. He called Tom to his office and said, 'I'm sending you to Chicago. Rest there at the weekend but don't come back without closing the deal on Monday. This is your last chance.'

Tom had less than two hours until his appointment and he was a wreck. He wiped his tears and sat with his back to the wall. He lit a second cigarette and inhaled deeply. The taste of burnt cigarette end was still there; he started to feel nauseous. He was thinking of death quite frequently these days but didn't know if that would be his salvation.

Room No 2: Steve

Steve was up very early. He had a whole two hours to spare before his meeting, but he had always liked to be prepared. He never ran late for anything. Not once, in his entire life. He was excited this morning because this was his first business trip outside New York. After 40 years in the civil service he still envied colleagues who travelled and stayed in hotels. Somehow, his newly appointed manager learned of Steve's desire and told him: 'Go ahead and travel a bit before you retire.' He'd come down to Atlanta to prepare for a meeting to be held the following month.

Steve was a finance specialist. After graduating from college, with his family's influence (and possibly their pressure), he started his job at the Ministry of Finance. Steve's father, stressed with his college fees, wanted him to work in the public sector with high job security. On the other hand, Steve did not have an ambitious personality. On graduation, he settled for a modest salary, even though, at that time, few people had a university diploma. In his career, he focused only on what he did, refraining from power and status struggles with others. Perhaps this was the reason why promotion eluded him and he had to work under less educated bosses. Despite the great discomfort of this situation, he always respected his superiors; he did what he was asked to do unquestioningly. His colleagues loved him because he never turned down any request for support. Those who thought him as a fainthearted character — a loser even — understood over time how good-hearted he was.

Steve also obeyed his parents faithfully. First, he got the job they wanted for him. Then he married the girl they wanted him to marry. His wife, Ashley, was a school teacher. He earned a bit and Ashley earned a bit, so they had a peaceful marriage, never needing anyone but each other. Yet, even though they never talked about it, they both envied people who led more colorful lives. Although they wanted to have two or even three children, they had only one girl, they named her Grace after Steve's mother. After finishing university, with her father's influence, Grace landed a job in the Ministry of Finance. She married Patrick, her colleague at the ministry. And although Patrick was unambitious, he was respectful and Steve loved him like a son.

Steve looked out of the hotel window. A busy schedule awaited him. 'What am I going to do around here for a whole week?" he asked himself. He was not used to being away from home, sleeping alone. Then he thought how monotonous his life was. Every day he lived was exactly the same as the previous one. Throughout his life he could not point to a single achievement of which he was proud, something he could share with his grandparents. Not one single reward except this trip. He felt the heaviness at being unable to make his mark on this world. 'Well,' he said to himself, 'My family and friends love me, that is more important than anything.' This was unconvincing but, at the age of 63, he felt that he lacked the courage to make a radical change in his lifestyle.

Room No 3: Caroline

Caroline Scully was a very popular person who'd clawed her way to the top of the advertising sector. She was born into a poor family, the youngest of four children. Although she was born in Lyon, her family moved to Paris when she was a baby. Her father worked for a long time in construction but following a serious accident at work, he and took a job as a doorman. After the accident, they moved to the basement of an apartment building where her father now worked. It was a wealthy suburb where she attended the same school as her rich neighbours. Initially the move was traumatic. She felt miserable, lonely and worthless. But at the same time, she became very ambitious and determined about her future. Her childhood was a misery but she wasn't going to let her youth be the same.

She wasn't a smart girl, but she worked hard day and night to catch up with the other kids. Although her primary school learning was unimpressive, her High School grades were outstanding. Then she got into the Faculty of Communication at a nearby university. Her studies and her future were more important to her than anything else. In her college years, she worked as an assistant to one of France's toughest advertisers. She never married. The truth is she never had the time for marriage. Except for necessary reading she had no hobbies. She saw music and dance as unproductive activities. She had done very well for herself, the company she set up at the age of thirty had become one of the biggest advertising agencies in the country.

She was in Chicago for a short, restful vacation. But she got up early as always and at the breakfast table began to examine her accountant's daily expenditure reports. A taxi expense for $30, from Megan, a sales representative, caught her attention. That lady got to the airport in a taxi?! Caroline could not tolerate such extravagance when she herself used public transportation. She immediately sent a tough e-mail to Megan and the accountant, demanding an explanation for this unnecessary expenditure. 'There's no peace, even on holiday,' she said to herself. She was angry. Then, for a moment, she felt some regret. 'Is it worth breaking people's heart for $30?' she asked herself. These kinds of thoughts had been crossing her mind quite often lately. She felt as if she was doing something wrong but she still couldn't control herself and just went her own way.

She took a dress from the suitcase and started to put it on. Despite her best efforts, she simply could not get into the blue skirt she bought in Italy. She'd put on weight recently. She was always starting a new diet. Yet she always ended up getting fatter and fatter. She blamed stress and the uncertainty at work for this but the real problem was her loveless life. Despite being a partner in one of the most important agencies in the country, her never-ending ambition to make more and more money condemned her to loneliness. She had nobody around her she could call a real friend. Even Elena, who'd helped her bring the company to this level, sold her shares at a knock-down price just to get away from her. She would have given up everything she had just to have a life like Elena's with its rich friendships. The sweet smile which appeared on people's faces when they heard Elena's name, just drove her mad. She always wondered why nobody blamed Elena even though she'd left the company halfway. She could imagine what people would have said about her if she had done such a thing.

Actually, she was trying to be close to people and establish good relationships with them. She seemed to care of their problems and really wished she had some people around who really loved her. But it just didn't happen. She couldn't break the ice between her and people. She considered adopting but then thought 'What if he doesn't love me and leaves when he grows up?' and gave up on this idea. Even her intention of adoption was selfish; as always, she was thinking of receiving rather than giving. And she could not see that the greatest obstacle to happiness was herself.

Room No 4: Caitlyn

Caitlyn and her husband Paul came to Chicago to celebrate their twenty-fifth wedding anniversary. Caitlyn had prepared a big surprise for Paul by reserving the same room in the hotel they'd stayed in during their honeymoon. Despite a number of restorations over time the hotel was basically the same. Almost everything was like in the old days. The nice thing was that Caitlyn still felt the way she did the day she was married.

But it wasn't just about feelings; her energy remained undiminished too. Again, she woke up at 6 o'clock in the morning and read halfway through the book she started during the trip. They decided to take a walk at 7 o'clock, if only Paul would wake up. The first night was a problem for Paul. Caitlyn could sleep throughout the trip, even on a bus, and she'd still be full of energy the next day. Paul wasn't built like that. When he visited a new place, he always found something to be concerned about. This time it was his pillow. Despite their agreement to go on an early morning walk he couldn't get himself out of the bed. 'Please, just one more hour,' he pleaded with his waiting wife. Caitlyn looked at him lovingly but there was a hint of a cynical smile at the corner of her mouth. She could never understand people, like her dear husband Paul, who slept for long hours, because five hours were more than enough for her.

For a moment, Caitlyn considered walking on her own instead of waiting. Then she changed her mind. She took her book and went out on the balcony. The view was exquisite. 'Look where we are now,' she said to herself. They had left twenty-five years behind. She recalled the days when they had to borrow money to buy her wedding dress and honeymoon. They started off in tiny flat. Their furniture was second hand and they painted the house themselves. For a long time, they didn't have bedroom furniture. Those were hard years. But somehow, they managed to overcome their difficulties together. Their sons Alan and Chandler were now at college. Caitlyn always said, 'I didn't raise my kids, they raised themselves'. This was because she believed that being a mother was like being a mediator. She expected the kids to handle their day-to-day affairs on their own, but would support them if they faced a challenge they could not overcome by themselves. For example, her kids washed and ironed their own clothes, prepared their own breakfasts. The same was true for school life. She did not attend the parents ' meetings at school and didn't even know the names of their teachers. Perhaps because of this, the boys took responsibility for their lives from an early age and without any special lessons they succeeded in getting into the best high schools available, entirely through their own efforts.

Caitlyn took the same perspective in her workplace. She gave responsibility to people, helped them to develop and prepared the necessary conditions for mutual achievement. She was always supportive when they encountered problems and found them right by her side when she was in difficulty. She saw the office as her second home and colleagues as her second family. For Caitlyn, work like play, was a fun and natural activity. She loved her job so much she didn't think she needed a vacation. She used the phrase 'change of air' instead of 'holiday' when she got away from work. And that was why they were in Chicago, for change of air.

She thought suddenly of her close friends. She even kept in contact with friends from her childhood days. She had a real closeness and connection with her friends. She could go to their houses out of the blue, whenever she wanted, and they could too. It was just last week that she hosted two friends at her house. They all slept in the living room together for three days. They could certainly have stayed at a hotel but Caitlyn insisted on spending as much as time together as possible. Next week there was the big reunion. All her high school friends were meeting for the thirtieth graduation year.

Caitlyn smiled at she thought of these. She felt fabulous and knew that this feeling had nothing to do with what she owned, the house, the car, the money in the bank or her status in the company. All her life, she invested in her family, friends and colleagues and enjoyed the satisfaction of achieving things together. She had a wonderful marriage, kids to be proud of, a job she loved and many great and trusted friends. 'What else can I ask for in life?' she thought. 'A little walk perhaps,' she said to herself and went inside to wake Paul.

4.

I think you'll find a piece of yourself in each of the four rooms. Now let's make a short analysis and decide which pieces to get rid of and which we should develop to achieve sustainable happiness.

One of the worst things that could happen to you in middle age is to get there and on looking up the word 'miserable' in the dictionary, finding a picture of you. No one wants to be miserable like Tom when they reach middle age. But we live in a very difficult world. Competition starts at primary school. Therefore, it is not at all easy to activate the happy chemicals in natural ways, with real achievements. On the other hand, the modern world offers us so many shortcuts to happiness. However, while these shortcuts may enrich our lives, when they aren't used within certain limits, they may cause us to end up like Tom.

Steve, on the other hand, chooses to work in a passive position in a public institution despite many alternatives after graduating from university. This choice provides him with job security that cannot be found in the private sector. However, his monotonous life within such a comfort zone causes his skills to get rusty over time. As a result, he loses courage to take initiative and action. He turns into a Loser (note the capital 'L') that has to work under people who have clearly been promoted to their level of incompetence, aren't as skilled as him and who cannot even express his thoughts. His choice brings him a peaceful life punctuated by the occasional smile but not exactly featuring outbursts of hilarity.

Like many others, Caroline also strives for money, power and prestige. In fact, she wants all these things to gain the love and appreciation of other people. But during this journey, she puts all her energy into her work and ignores her friends. She sees the people she works with as instruments to help reach her personal goals. She expects them to do what she says and in return meets their financial expectations. In this way, she makes people dependent on her. However, she feels that this relationship based on self interest will end and she will not have anyone around, the moment she falls off her power pedestal. She tries to close this gap of trust by attaining more power and prestige. Her choice makes her lonelier than a one-woman Mexican wave.

Actually, Caroline wants to be loved by people and gain their appreciation just like Elena. However, she is trying to achieve this not by establishing superiority over them or using her influence but by strengthening them and contributing to their development. She doesn't leave them alone in their difficult moments. Almost everyone, from her children to her colleagues, respond to Caitlyne approach in the same away. The resulting synergy allows Caitlyne to easily overcome problems she cannot tackle on her own. Moreover, thanks to the intimate relationships that Caitlyne has established with her friends, she feels secure, happy and at peace, all at the same time.

Life is about choices. Should we go to the right or to the left? Should we walk or run? Or, if you're a skier, do you zig? Or zag? Sometimes our decisions bring about good results but other things may deteriorate because of them. But a decision that we will make independently from all other things determines how we will feel in the journey to success, as well as the results we will achieve: Will we proceed alone or together?

Going alone can speed us up. We can achieve success and happiness very quickly yet this kind of dopamine based happiness doesn't last very long and the journey is awfully stressful. Therefore, if we want to enjoy the journey and make our happiness permanent, we need to get serotonin and oxytocin supplements, in other words, we need to move forward together with other people.

Notes

FOREWORD

1. Lindstrom, M. (2010). Buyology: Truth and Lies About Why We Buy. New York: Crown Business.

INTRODUCTION - JOY.OLOGY: GENERAL OVERVIEW

1. Frankl V.E. (2009). Man's Search for Meaning. New York: Beacon Press.

2. He is the founder of 3rd Viennese School. Viktor Frankl, one of the most important names of existential therapy, has introduced Logotherapy (therapy focused on meaning) which is based on his theory that he developed during his 4 years of imprisonment in German concentration camps in Poland during World War II.

3. The feeling we call "happiness" is created by hormones that are called dopamine, serotonin, endorphin and oxytocin. When we experience any incident that contributes to our survival and continuation of mankind, our brain rewards us by triggering one or more of these hormones. The feelings that each hormone evokes are different from each other: Dopamine is the success hormone, serotonin is the status hormone, oxytocin is the trust hormone and endorphin is the hormone for masking physical pain.

4. Breuning L. G. (2015). Habits of a Happy Brain: Retrain Your Brain to Boost Your Serotonin, Dopamine, Oxytocin, & Endorphin Levels, Avon: Adams Media.

5. Dickinson A, Balleine B. (2008) Hedonics: The Cognitive-motivational Interface. Incuding: Kringelbach ML, Berridge KC, editors. Pleasures of the Brain. Oxford, UK: Oxford University Press.

6. Talbott S. (2007). The Cortisol Connection: Why Stress Makes You Fat and Ruins Your Health and What You Can Do About It. Alemeda: Hounter House.

7. Iversen L., Iversen S., Dunnett S., Bjorklund A. (2010). Dopamine Handbook. New York: Oxford University Press.

8. Breuning L. G. (2008). I, Mammal: Why Your Brain Links Status and Happiness. California: Inner Mammal Institute.

9. Bloom W. (2011). The Endorphin Effect: A Breakthrough Strategy for Holistic Health and Spiritual Wellbeing. Oakland: Little, Brown.

10. Moberg K. U. (2003). The Oxytocin Factor: Tapping the Hormone of Calm, Love and Healing. Cambridge: Da Capo Press.

11. Harari Y.N. (2015). Sapiens: A Brief History of Humankind. New York. Harper Collins.

12. Ugel E. (2009). Money for Nothing: One Man's Journey through the Dark Side of Lottery Millions. New York. Harper Collins.

13. The man who won the lottery for three times, for details of the story: "Waiting for stroke of luck for the 4th time" Sabah newspaper, 24.12.2010. Online: goo.gl/oesn7t

14. To review all comments about lottery millionaires, see: "Winning the lottery: Does it guarantee happiness?" CNN. 07.01.2011. Online: goo.gl/SHM5Iv

15. Langheim L. (2008). Effects of Stress - Cerebral Blood Flow Velocity, Salivary Cortisol, and Subjective State. VDM Verlag.

16. Milosevic I., McCabe R. (2015). Phobias: The Psychology of Irrational Fear. Santa Barbara: Greenwood.

17. Talbott S., Skolnik H. (2004). The Cortisol Connection Diet: The Breakthrough Program to Control Stress and Lose Weight. Berkeley C.A.: Publishers Group West.

18. Lne N. (2015). The Vital Question: Energy, Evolution, and the Origins of Complex Life. New York: W. W. Norton & Company.

19. Angel L. J. (1984). "Health as a crucial factor in the changes from hunting to developed farming in the eastern Mediterranean", Proceedings of meeting on Paleopathology at the Origins of Agriculture: 51–73

20. Volkow N.D., Fowler S., Wang G.J. (2007). "Dopamine in Drug Abuse and Addiction Results of Imaging Studies and Treatment Implications" Arch Neurol: 64 (11), 1575-1579.

21. The classification of "primitive brain and rational brain" is based on Nobel Prize winner psychologist Daniel Kahneman's classification for thinking "System 1: Fast Thinking and System 2: Slow Thinking" which is included in his book "Thinking, Fast and Slow". For detailed information,

please see: Kahneman D. (2013). Thinking, Fast and Slow. New York: Farrar, Straus and Giroux.

22. Han, D.H., Lee, Y.S., Yang, K. (2007). "Dopamine Genes and Reward Dependence in Adolescents with Excessive Internet Video Game Play", Journal of Addiction Medicine: 1 (3), 133-138.

23. Badt, K. (2013). Mirror Neurons and Why We Love Cinema: A Conversation with Vittorio Gallese and Michele Guerra in Parma. The Huffington Post.

24. Waddington C.H. (1957). The Strategy of the Gene, London: George Allen & Unwin.

25. Sigmund F. (1989). The Psychopathology of Everyday Life. New York: W. W. Norton.

26. For detailed information on how the human brain changes with learning, see: Rakic, P. (January 2002). "Neurogenesis in adult primate neocortex: an evaluation of the evidence". Nature Reviews Neuroscience. 3 (1): 65–71. Pascual-Leone A.; Amedi A.; Fregni F.; Merabet L. B. (2005). "The plastic human brain cortex". Annual Review of Neuroscience. 28: 377–401. Keller TA, Just MA (January 2016). "Structural and functional neuroplasticity in human learning of spatial routes". Neuroimage. 125: 256–266. Doidge, Norman (2007). The Brain that Changes Itself. Penguin Books. Leaf C. (2013). Switch on Your Brain: The Key to Peak Happiness, Thinking, and Health, Michigan: Baker Books.

CHAPTER 1: WHO HAS CONTROL?

1. The story explaining how limited control we have over our own lives is based on the interviews given by Prof. Dr. Canan Karatay to the press and on the news about the subject. For details see: NTV 31 October 2013 "Canan Karatay was defrauded" Online: goo.gl/Zl9Skp YouTube "Canan Karatay was also defrauded" Online: goo.gl/rRR0KT Sabah newspaper 31 October Ekim 2013 "Prof.Dr. Canan Karatay has been defrauded" Online goo.gl/S7jlOE"

2. Milliyet Newspaper 15 October 2015 "Law professor lost 4.5 million to fraud" Online: goo.gl/R4W98D

3. Sabah Newspaper 8 November 2013 "The top professor was also defrauded" Online: goo.gl/o2fwG2

4. Haber7com 5 November 2013 "He was defrauded just like Canan Karatay" Online: goo.gl/NJn8Vw

5. Sabah newspaper 12 Nisan 2013 "He drew a bank loan to give money to the defrauder!" Online: goo.gl/wBl2T2

6. Abrahams P. (2015). How the Brain Works. New York: Metro Books.

7. Kahneman D. (2013). Thinking, Fast and Slow. New York: Farrar, Straus and Giroux.

8. Eagleman D. (2012). Incognito: The Secret Lives of the Brain. New York: Vintage Publishing.

9. Montague, P.R., McClure S.M., Li J., Tomlin D., Cypert K.S., Montague L. (2004). "Neural Correlates of Behavioral Preference for Culturally Familiar Drinks". Neuron. 44 (2): 379–387.

10. To see the news about Aylan Kurdi who drowned in Bodrum: International "Image of 3-year-old who washed ashore underscores Europe's refugee crisis" Online: https://goo.gl/HdGls9, BBC News "Migrant crisis: Photo of drowned boy sparks outcry" Online: http://goo.gl/s6sVGq, The New York Times, "Brutal Images of Syrian Boy Drowned Off Turkey Must Be Seen, Activists Say" Online: http://goo.gl/qrLaa8, Independent, "Aylan Kurdi's story: How a small Syrian child came to be washed up on a beach in Turkey" Online: http://goo.gl/IfktUk, The Washington Post, "A dead baby becomes the most tragic symbol yet of the Mediterranean refugee crisis" Online: http://goo.gl/Glkj00

11. See the details of the #refugeeswelcome campaign initiated by Independent after the death of Aylan Kurdi and the statements of Angela Merkel, David Cameron, François Hollande, George Osborne, Nigel Farage: Independent 3 October 2015 "Refugee crisis live: Aylan Kurdi's death drives international pressure for Europe to act as people smugglers arrested in Turkey" Online: http://goo.gl/PnjBUB

12. Skinner, S. K., Reilly, W. K. (1989). The Exxon Valdez Oil Spill: A Report to the President. National Response Team.

13. This research was taken from Daniel Kahneman's book "Thinking, Fast and Slow."

14. Elite Daily 25 March 2015. "The Odds of A Plane Crash Are One In 11 Million, Yet You're Still Afraid" Online: goo.gl/yGRJqf

15. The Guardian 5 October 2011 "September 11's indirect toll: road deaths linked to fearful flyers" Online: goo.gl/7HggMc

16. CNN "September 11, 2001: Background and timeline of the attacks" Online: goo.gl/TGD9q7

17. Rock D. (2009). Your Brain at Work: Strategies for Overcoming Distraction, Regaining Focus, and Working Smarter All Day Long. New York: Harper Collins.

18. O'Connor R. (2015). Rewire: Change Your Brain to Break Bad Habits, Overcome Addictions, Conquer Self-Destructive Behavior. New York: Random House.

19. The Telegraph 30 April 2008. Motorists bugged by insects. Online: goo.gl/eySZbh

20. Jules Mazarin (July 14, 1602 - March 9, 1661), an Italian politician who became the de facto leader of France, ruled the country after the death of Cardinal Richelieu. He used religion as a political tool and fought with fanatic Catholic movements even though he was raised from the Italian Church. Mazarin ruled France at a time when the kings couldn't function efficiently and set the foundation for Louis XIV future power. Encouraged by the death of Mazarin, Louis removed his mother's rights over the state and has taken the power in his hands. For more information, see: Dethan, G. (1991). "Mazarin, Jules, Cardinal" in The New Encyclopedia Britannica, volume 7, p. 979.

21. To summarize the research results: Although we believe that we make our choices consciously, almost all our decisions are taken by our primitive brain. Our rational brain spends a great deal of time and energy to generate justifications for decisions taken by our primitive brain. And this is not only limited to trivial issues; this is how we make the serious decisions which affect our lives and our loved ones. Even the smallest sign that activate our primitive brain can make the concrete facts worthless yet we are often unaware of this situation and in fact, even if we realize it, not much changes.

CHAPTER 2: CAN I CHANGE?

1. Woollett K., Maguire EA. (2009). "Navigational expertise may compromise anterograde associative memory". Neuropsychologia. 47(4):1088-95.

2. For more information about the physical change that is experienced in the brain with learning: Doidge N. (2007). The Brain That Changes Itself: Stories of Personal Triumph from the Frontiers of Brain Science. New York: Penguin Books. Falk, D.; Lepore, F. E.; Noe, A. (2012). "The cerebral cortex of Albert Einstein: A description and preliminary analysis of unpublished photographs". Brain. 136 (4): 1304–27. Sweeney M.S. (2009). Brain: The

Complete Mind: How It Develops, How It Works, and How to Keep It Sharp. New York: National Geographic.

3. Neurons in different regions of the brain must communicate with each other for a certain feeling, thought or behavior to occur. This communication takes place with electrochemical signals sent over neural networks between neurons. Each time these warnings are sent out, the channels to which the warning travels expand; a physical change occurs. This makes the transition of the signal from one point to another easier, prevents any possible deviation and becomes automatic. This is how we learn and form our habits. We need to establish new links between neurons to change our habits. However, our brain does not want to create new links when there are existing ones available and it is difficult to change habits because the brain always chooses the easy way. When we develop an alternative way or a habit, we will have a hard time in the beginning however as we repeat the newly forming habit, the links expand whereas the other links weaken over time. In this way, while certain points of our brain are physically shrinking, new formations come into existence.

4. Eagleman, D. (2015). The Brain: The Story of You. New York: Pantheon Books.

5. Kahneman D. (2013). Thinking, Fast and Slow. New York: Farrar, Straus and Giroux.

6. Doidge N. (2007). The Brain That Changes Itself: Stories of Personal Triumph from the Frontiers of Brain Science. New York: Penguin Books.

7. Falk, D.; Lepore, F. E.; Noe, A. (2012). "The cerebral cortex of Albert Einstein: A description and preliminary analysis of unpublished photographs". Brain. 136 (4): 1304–27.

8. Sweeney M.S. (2009). Brain: The Complete Mind: How It Develops, How It Works, and How to Keep It Sharp. New York: National Geographic.

9. Duhigg C. (2014). The Power of Habit: Why We Do What We Do in Life and Business. New York: Random House.

CHAPTER 3: I CAN'T BE HAPPY

1."Fight or flight reaction": All mammals, including humans, respond to the threats they face with a reaction called "fight or flight". This is a protective response for living things and activates physical reactions such as increase in breathing frequency, number of heart beats and the level of tension in the muscles. Fight or flight reaction is critical for evolution and is related to "survival". The "fight or flight" is useful in cases of sudden dangers and when fast and effective action is required (for example, when someone is attacked on the street). However, there are times when this reaction is not appropriate or disproportionate. In our world today, there are many dangers or problems that are inherently long-lasting (such as financial stress due to lack of job security). In such situations, it is not possible to solve the problem quickly by escaping it or by instant elimination. That's why, in the modern world, the "fight or flight" reaction does not only become useless, but on the contrary, it has harmful implications for our body and spiritual health.

2. For detailed information about "fight or flight" reaction, see: Jansen, A., Nguyen, X., Karpitsky, V., Mettenleiter, M. (1995). "Central Command Neurons of the Sympathetic Nervous System: Basis of the Fight-or-Flight Response". Science Magazine. (270): 5236. Goldstein, D.; Kopin, I. (2007). "Evolution of concepts of stress". Stress. 10 (2): 109–20. Sapolsky, R. M., (1994). Why Zebras Don't Get Ulcers. New York: W.H. Freeman and Company.

3. Schmidt, A., Thews, G. (1989). "Autonomic Nervous System". inc. Janig, W. Human Physiology (2 ed.). New York: Springer-Verlag. 333–370.

4. For more information about the structure and functions of the hippocampus, see: Duvernoy, H., Cattin F., Risold P. (2013). The Human Hippocampus: Functional Anatomy, Vascularization and Serial Sections with MRI, New York: Springer.

5. For more detailed information about the structure and functions of the amygdala: Bzdok D, Laird A, Zilles K, Fox PT, Eickhoff S. (2012). An investigation of the structural, connectional and functional sub-specialization in the human amygdala. Human Brain Mapping.

6. Tancredi L. (2004). Hardwired Behavior: What Neuroscience Reveals about Morality, Cambridge: Cambridge University Press.

7. Goldstein, D., Kopin, I (2007). "Evolution of concepts of stress". Stress. 10 (2): 109–20.

8. Bear M.F., Connors B.W., Paradiso M.A. (2016). Neuroscience: Exploring the Brain. New York: Wolters Kluwer.

9. Lovallo R.W. (2015). Stress and Health: Biological and Psychological Interactions. Los Angeles: Sage.

10. Sapolsky R.M. (2004). Why Zebras Don't Get Ulcers. New York: Henry Holt and Company.

11. Wingo M. (2016). The Impact of the human stress response: The biological origins and solutions to human stress. Texas: Roxwell Waterhouse.

12. Schmidt, A., Thews, G. (1989). "Autonomic Nervous System". inc. W. Human Physiology (2 ed.). New York: Springer-Verlag. 333–370.

13. Hanson R. (2013). Hardwiring Happiness: The New Brain Science of Contentment, Calm, and Confidence. New York: Random House.

14. Bingaman K.A. (2014). The Power of Neuroplasticity for Pastoral and Spiritual Care. Plymouth, Lexington Books.

15. Taken from Alison Ledgerwood's TEDx talk titled "Getting Stuck in the Negatives" dated January 22, 2013. Online: http://goo.gl/9WMCvK

16. Field T, Hernandez-Reif M, Diego M, Schanberg S, Kuhn C (2005). "Cortisol decreases and serotonin and dopamine increase following massage therapy". Int. J. Neurosci. 115 (10): 1397–413.

17. Quervain DJ, Roozendaal B, Nitsch RM, McGaugh JL, Hock C (April 2000). "Acute cortisone administration impairs retrieval of long-term declarative memory in humans". Nat. Neurosci. 3 (4): 313–4.

18. Wolkowitz O.M., Rothschild A. J. Psychoneuroendocrinology: The Scientific Basis of Clinical Practice, Washington: American Psychiatric Publishing.

19. Ebrecht M, Hextall J, Kirtley LG, Taylor A, Dyson M, Weinman J (2004). "Perceived stress and cortisol levels predict speed of wound healing in healthy male adults". Psychoneuroendocrinology. 29 (6): 798–809.

20. Sapolsky R.M. (2004). Why Zebras Don't Get Ulcers. New York: Henry Holt and Company.

21. Chiu HK, Tsai EC, Juneja R, (2007). "Equivalent insulin resistance". Diabetes Research and Clinical Practice. PubMed. 77: 237–44.

22. Padgett, David; Glaser, R (August 2003). "How stress influences the immune response". Trends in Immunology. 24 (8): 444–448.

23. Nishiyama K., Johnson J.V. (1997). "Karoshi-Death from overwork: Occupational health consequences of the Japanese production management". International Journal of Health Services.

24. Talbott S., Kraemer W. (2007). The Cortisol Connection: Why Stress Makes You Fat and Ruins Your Health, Berkeley: Group West.

25. Lovallo R.W. (2015). Stress and Health: Biological and Psychological Interactions. Los Angeles: Sage.

26. Spoor, S. T., Bekker, M. H., van Strien, T., van Heck, G. L. (2007). "Relations between negative affect, coping, and emotional eating". Appetite. 48: 368–376.

27. Sapolsky R.M. (2004). Why Zebras Don't Get Ulcers. New York: Henry Holt and Company.

28. Seward B.L. (2014). Managing Stress: Principles and Strategies for Health and Well-Being. New York: Jones & Bartlett Learning.

29. Burkeman O. (2013). The Antidote: Happiness for People Who Can't Stand Positive Thinking. New York: Farrar, Straus and Giroux.

30. Compton W.C., Hoffman E. (2012). Positive Psychology: The Science of Happiness and Flourishing. New York: Cengage Learning.

31. The Candle Experiment was taken from the TED talk titled "The puzzle of motivation" by Daniel Pink on June 7, 2009. Online: goo.gl/4jUJ9u

32. Glenville M. (2006). Mastering Cortisol: Stop Your Body's Stress Hormone from Making You Fat Around the Middle. Berkeley: Ulyses Press.

33. McAuley MT, Kenny RA, Kirkwood TB, Wilkinson DJ, Jones JJ, Miller VM (2009). "A mathematical model of aging-related and cortisol induced hippocampal dysfunction". BMC Neurosci. 10: 26.

34. Greenberg J. (2012) Comprehensive Stress Management. New York: McGraw Hill.

35. Schneiderman, N., Ironson, G., Siegel, S. D. (2005). "Stress and health: psychological, behavioral, and biological determinants". Annual Review of Clinical Psychology. 1: 607–628.

36. Marucha P.T., Kiecolt-Glaser J.K., Favagehi M. (1998). "Mucosal wound healing is impaired by examination stress". Psychosom Med. 60 (3): 362–5.

37. We know that it does not make sense to feel sorry for things we cannot change but we still have difficulty in removing such negativities from our minds. Our unhappiness often takes over our happiness.

CHAPTER 4: I DID IT

1. Dopamine is a naturally produced chemical in our body. It acts as a neurotransmitter, that is, it provides communication between neurons. Dopamine is often referred to as "hormone of happiness" like serotonin. In addition to creating happiness, dopamine also performs many functions such as

movement, reward, behavior, attention, and learning. In lack of dopamine, Parkinson's disease occurs. Increase of dopamine by using drugs or smoking results in addiction. In case of an incident that will contribute to survival and continuation of our kind, our brain releases dopamine. In this way, the brain prompts the person to repeat the same behavior.

2. Iversen L., Iversen S., Dunnett S., Björklund A. (2010). Dopamine Handbook. New York: Oxford University Press.

3. Bray, G. A. (2011). A Guide to Obesity and the Metabolic Syndrome: Origins and Treatment, Boca Raton: Taylor and Francis Group.

4. For details about the changes in expectations regarding Life Expectancy over the centuries: "Life expectancy" Wikipedia, Online: goo.gl/zgDTAW

5. Ringo A. (2013). "Why Do Some Brains Enjoy Fear?" The Atlantic Online: goo.gl/c5I78G

6. Salimpoor V. N. Benovoy M., Larcher K. (2011) "Anatomically distinct dopamine release during anticipation and experience of peak emotion to music" Nature Neuroscience: 14, 257–262.

7. Green C. S., Bavelier D. (2004). The Cognitive Neuroscience of Video Games. Harvard University Papers. Online: goo.gl/0aUoOD

8. Jabr F. (2012). "How the Brain Gets Addicted to Gambling" Scientific American. Online: goo.gl/wEyUFn

9. Brody, A.L., Olmstead R.E., Edythe D. (2004). "Smoking-Induced Ventral Striatum Dopamine Release." Am J Psychiatry 161:7, 1211-1218.

10. Boileau S., Assaad J., Pihl R. (2003). Alcohol Promotes Dopamine Release in the Human Nucleus Accumbens. Synapse 49. 226–231.

11. Reuptake inhibitors, norepinephrine and dopamine, which are called NDRIs: bupropion (Wellbutrin, Aplenzin, Forfivo XL) are in this category.

12. Breuning L. G. (2015). Habits of a Happy Brain: Retrain Your Brain to Boost Your Serotonin, Dopamine, Oxytocin, & Endorphin Levels, Avon: Adams Media.

13. Csikszentmihalyi M. (2008). Flow: The Psychology of Optimal Experience. New York: Harper Perennial.

14. Arely D. (2010). Predictably Irrational: The Hidden Forces That Shape Our Decisions. New York: Harper Perennial.

15. Kahneman D. (2013). Thinking, Fast and Slow. New York: Farrar, Straus and Giroux.

16. Seligman M. E. (2004). Authentic Happiness: Using the New Positive Psychology to Realize Your Potential for Lasting Fulfillment. New York: Atria Books.

17. Dahl M. (2016). "A Classic Psychology Study on Why Winning the Lottery Won't Make You Happier" Science of Us Online: goo.gl/FkLYwO

18. Life is a process in which we run from one anxiety to the other and the same goes for our desires. This is not to say we shouldn't consider our worries or try to satisfy our desires. However, we must be aware that, although our goals promise us that once we succeeded, we will be able to stop and rest, this is far from truth. The car we have, like all the other things we possess, will melt away in the material background of our lives. After a while its presence will not even be noticed.

19. Iversen L., Iversen S., Dunnett S., Björklund A. (2010). Dopamine Handbook. New York: Oxford University Press.

20. Luthar S. S. (2013). "The Problem with Rich Kids" Psychology Today. Online: goo.gl/NcJhSs

21. For more about the tragedies of the kids from rich families, see: Sunburn J. (2012) "Why Suicides Are More Common in Richer Neighborhoods" Time. Online: goo.gl/JmLfSp Jacobs D. (2013). "Why Family Wealth Is A Curse" Forbes Online: goo.gl/V1d1EJ

22. For more detailed information about internalizing happiness and making it last, see: Hanson R. (2013). Hardwiring Happiness: The New Brain Science of Contentment, Calm, and Confidence. New York: Harmony.

23. Lee J. (2014). Your Brain Electric: Everything you need to know about optimising neurotransmitters including serotonin, dopamine and noradrenaline. New York: CreateSpace.

24. For other examples that illustrate the logic of the irrational, see: Ariely D. (2011). The Upside of Irrationality: The Unexpected Benefits of Defying Logic. New York: Harper Perennial.

25. Nelson L.F., Meyvis T. (2008) Interrupted Consumption: Disrupting Adaptation to Hedonic Experiences. Journal of Marketing Research: 45/6, 654-664.

26. The cerebral cortex is the region of the brain where most of the dopamine sensitive neurons function. Source: Susan Ayers, Richard de Visser (2011). Psychology for Medicine, Sage Publications,154.

27. Dan Ariely is a professor of Behavioral Economics at Duke University. He carries out studies on cognitive neurology and economics in Fuqua Faculty of Business. He has a doctorate degree in both cognitive psychology and business administration.

28. Camus A., O'Brien J. (1991). The Myth of Sisyphus and Other Essays, New York. Vintage.

29. Dobelli R. (2014). The Art of Thinking Clearly. New York: Harper Paperbacks.

30. Csikszentmihalyi M. (2008). Flow: The Psychology of Optimal Experience. New York: Harper Perennial.

31. We all believe that by reaching success and having things, we can attain satisfaction that lasts. We think that we will reach the flat, stable and vast platforms after climbing the steep and difficult slopes of happiness. And that, constant satisfaction awaits us at the end of that slope. However, we are never reminded of this: we will be descending shortly after we reach the peak and find ourselves again on the ground, in the soil of anxiety and desire.

CHAPTER 5: I WANT RESPECT

1. Kalueff A., LaPorte J. L. (2010) Experimental Models in Serotonin Transporter Research New York: Cambridge University Press.

2. Baumel S. (1997) Serotonin. Connecticut: Keats Publishing.

3. Giovanni G., Matteo V., Esposito E. (2008). Serotonin-Dopamine Interaction: Experimental Evidence and Therapeutic Relevance. New York: Elsevier Science

4. Game of Thrones is a TV series created by David Benioff and D. B. Weiss. It is adapted from George Martin's series of epic fantasy novels "A Song of Ice and Fire" and takes its name from the first book in the series. For more information about Games of Thrones, see: goo.gl/1YEQfJ

5. The discussion about status in this chapter was compiled from Alain de Button's book, "Status Anxiety". For more information about the sources of status anxiety and what can be done to overcome, see Button A. (2005). Status Anxiety. New York: Vintage Books.

6. Breuning L.G. (2011). I, Mammal: How to Make Peace with the Animal Urge for Social Power. California: Inner Mammal Institute.

7. Smith A. (2013). The Theory of Moral Sentiments. New York: Economic Classics. Quoted by: Button A. (2005). Status Anxiety. New York: Vintage Books.

8. James W. (1950). The Principles of Psychology. Dover Books. Quoted by: Button A. (2005). Status Anxiety. New York: Vintage Books.

9. Raven, M., Depression and antidepressants in Australia and beyond - a critical public health analysis, Doctor of Philosophy thesis, Faculty of Arts, University of Wollongong, 2012.

10. Heitler S. (2011). "Antidotes to Boredom: Why Shopping is Fun". Psychology Today. Online: goo.gl/zX0t2r

11. O'connor M.C. (2012) "Facebook's secret design sauce? It's serotonin" ZDNet. Online: goo.gl/krvi9z

12. Andrews CM, Lucki I. (2001). "Effects of cocaine on extracellular dopamine and serotonin levels in the nucleus accumbens." Psychopharmacology (Berl). 155(3): 221-9.

13. Rousseau J.J. (2012). Discourse on the Origin and the Foundations of Inequality Among Men. New York: Hackett Publishing Company.

14. Button A. (2005). Status Anxiety. New York: Vintage Books.

15. Covey S. (1989). The 7 Habits of Highly Effective People: Powerful Lessons in Personal Change. New York: Simon & Schuster.

16. For additional information about serotonin, see: Kay K., Shipman C. (2014). The Confidence Code: The Science and Art of Self-Assurance. New York: Harper Business. Hart C. (2008). Secrets of Serotonin, Revised Edition: The Natural Hormone That Curbs Food and Alcohol Cravings, Reduces Pain, and Elevates Your Mood. New York: Lynn Sonberg Books. Maximino C. (2012). Serotonin and Anxiety: Neuroanatomical, Pharmacological, and Functional Aspects. New York: SpringerBriefs.

CHAPTER 6: YES, I FEEL GOOD

1. Jansen, A., Nguyen, X., Karpitsky, V., Mettenleiter, M. (1995). "Central Command Neurons of the Sympathetic Nervous System: Basis of the Fight-or-Flight Response". Science Magazine. (270): 5236.

2. Ingledew D., Markland D. (2008). "The role of motives in exercise participation". Psychology & Health. 23, 7, 807-828.

3. Baby M., Blumenthal J. (2000). "Exercise Treatment for Major Depression: Maintenance of Therapeutic Benefit at 10 Months" Psychosomatic Medicine 62:633–638.

4. Broocks A., Bandelow B., Pekrun G. (1998). "Comparison of aerobic exercise, clomipramine, and placebo in the treatment of panic disorder" The American Journal Psychiatry. 155(5):603-9.

5. Trivedi M.H., Greer T.L., Grannemann B.D. (2006). "Exercise as an augmentation strategy for treatment of major depression." Journal of Psychiatric Practice 12(4):205-13.

6. Trivedi M.H., Greer T.L., Church T.S., Carmody T.J. (2011). "Exercise as an augmentation treatment for nonremitted major depressive disorder: a randomized, parallel dose comparison". Journal of Clinical Psychiatry. 72(5):677-84.

7. O'Connor A. (2012). "Exercise May Ease Depression in Heart Failure Patients". Exercise and the Brain Collection. New York: New York Times Company.

8. Ratey J.J. (2008). Spark. New York: Little, Beown and Company.

9. Exercise and the Brain. (2015). TBook Collections. New York: The New York Times Company.

10. Nietzsche F. (2013). Twilight of the Idols: Sis Publications.

11. Natali C., Hutchinson D.S. (2013). Aristotle: His Life and School Kindle Edition. New Jersey: Princeton University Press.

12. Reynolds, G. (2011). "How Exercise Benefits the Brain" Exercise and the Brain Collection. New York: New York Times Company.

13. Hamblin J. (2014). "Exercise Is ADHD Medication" The Atlantic. Online: goo.gl/v8NAW7

14. Hopkins M.E., Davis F.C., van Tieghem M., Bucci D. (2012). "Differential Effects of Acute and Regular Physical Exercise on Cognition and Affect". Neuroscience. 26; 215: 59–68.

15. Gow A., Bastin M.E., Munoz S. (2012). "Neuroprotective lifestyles and the aging brain: activity, atrophy, and white matter integrity." Neurology. 23; 79(17):1802-8.

16. Head D., Bugg J.M., Goate A.M., Fagan AM (2012). "Exercise Engagement as a Moderator of the Effects of APOE Genotype on Amyloid Deposition". Archives of Neurology 69(5):636-43.

17. DeFina L.F., Willis B.L., Radford N.B. (2013) "The Association Between Midlife Cardiorespiratory Fitness Levels and Later-Life Dementia. A Cohort Study." Annals of Internal Medicine. 158(3): 162–168.

18. Rhodes J.S., Kohman R.A., DeYoung E.K. (2012). "Wheel running attenuates microglia proliferation and increases expression of a proneurogenic phenotype in the hippocampus of aged mice." Brain, Behavior, and Immunity. 26: 803-810.

19. Tali K., Chunyan Y., and Henriette van P. (2011). Endurance factors improve hippocampal neurogenesis and spatial memory in mice. Learning Memory. 18(2): 103–107.

20. Beck D., Beck J. (1987). Pleasure Connection: How Endorphins Affect Our Health and Happiness. Synthesis.

21. Boom, W. (2001). The Endorphin Effect: A Breakthrough Strategy for Holistic Health and Spiritual Wellbeing. London: Hachette Digital.

22. McKenna P. (2009). Control Stress Stop Worrying and Feel Good Now! London: Bantam Press.

23. Breuning L. G. (2015). Habits of a Happy Brain: Retrain Your Brain to Boost Your Serotonin, Dopamine, Oxytocin, & Endorphin Levels, Avon: Adams Media.

24. Research shows that the act of laughing triggers the release of endorphin just like exercising. You may not be able to make sense of how your body reacts watching a funny movie and running a marathon in similar ways. Yet, they do have a common point. "Pain!" Especially in the abdominal region, contractions and relaxations are actually so painful that even endorphin may be inadequate at times. You have certainly experienced such moments when you laugh so hard that you beg the person who makes you laugh to stop or try to leave the place. In this respect, laughing can be as tiring, painful and at the same time as relaxing as a high-tempo workout. This is why the audiences say, "we died laughing" after a good comedy film or stand up show: Laughter is tiring, painful and endorphin triggered by laughter feels fabulous.

25. Many people may first think of adrenaline, before endorphin, when physical activity, performance and enthusiasm are mentioned. However, adrenaline is a chemical designed to meet the sudden energy need of our bodies and it is triggered along with cortisol. For example, during bungee jumping, our rational brain knows that we are safe; however, the primitive brain is unaware of this since it learns from experience. Adrenaline, along with high amounts of cortisol, is also released into the blood when you fall,

and some people enjoy this energy burst very much. In short, adrenaline is not a hormone for happiness; it provides instantaneous stimulation at high levels and that's why it is not included in this book.

26. Kancel C. (2016). Happy Brain: Boost Your Dopamine, Serotonin, Oxytocin & Other Neurotransmitters Naturally, Improve Your Focus and Brain Functions. Live & Life Publishing.

CHAPTER 7: SO GLAD, I HAVE YOU

1. For more information on the Roseto Case which observes the effects of social relations on human health, see: Bruhn J.B., Wolf S., Wolff R. (2003). The Roseto Story: An Anatomy of Health. Oklahoma: University of Oklahoma Press. Ve Wolf S., Bruhn J.G. (1998). The Power of Clan: The Influence of Human Relationships on Heart Disease. New York: Transaction Publishers.

2. Poulin M.J., Brown S.L., Dillard A.J., Smith D.M. (2013). "Giving to others and the association between stress and mortality" American Journal of Public Health. 103, 9, 1649-1655.

3. For more information about the Dead Sea and the Galilee Seas, see: Wikipedia. Online: https://goo.gl/clQs6Q ve https://goo.gl/72Osws

4. Shenk J.F. (2009). "What Makes Us Happy?" The Atlantic. Mart, 23-44.

5. Vaillant, G., Mukamal K. (2001). Successful Aging. American Journal of Psychiatry, 158:839–847.

6. Stossel S. (2013). "What Makes Us Happy, Revisited. A new look at the famous Harvard study of what makes people thrive" May 55-56.

7. Moberg K.U., Francis R. (2003). The Oxytocin Factor: Tapping The Hormone Of Calm, Love, And Healing. Cambridge: Da Capo Press.

8. Zak P.J. (2012). The Moral Molecule: How Trust Works New York: Plume.

9. Cialdini R.B. (2009). Influence: The Psychology of Persuasion. New York: HarperCollins.

10. Simon. S. (2009). Start with Why: How Great Leaders Inspire Everyone to Take Action. New York: Portfolio.

11. Covey, S. (2006). The Speed of Trust: The One Thing that Changes Everything. New York: Free Press.

12. Ganten D., Pfaff D., Burbach J.P. (1986). Neurobiology of Oxytocin. New York: Springer.

13. Blendon, R. J., DesRoches, C. M., Brodie, M., Benson, J. M., Rosen, A. B. (2002). "Views of practicing physicians and the public on medical errors". New England Journal of Medicine, 347(24), 1933-1940.

14. Verghese, A., Brady, E., Kapur, C. C., & Horwitz, R. I. (2011). The bedside evaluation: ritual and reason. Annals of internal medicine, 155(8), 550-553.

15. Verghese, A. (2009). A touch of sense. Health Affairs, 28(4), 1177-1182.

16. Dunn, E., Norton M. Happy Money: The Science of Happier Spending. New York: Simon & Schuster.

17. Helliwell, J., Huang, H., Wang, S. (2016). Word Happiness Report. Canadian Institute for Advanced Research, Gallup Organization.

18. Kuchinskas, S. (2009). The Chemistry of Connection: How the Oxytocin Response Can Help You Find Trust, Intimacy, and Love. New York: New Harbinger Publications.

19. Anderson E. (2015). Advances in Oxytocin Research. New York: Nova Science Publishers.

20. Anonymous Alcoholics (AA) is an organization founded in America in 1936. To join the organization, which has more than two million members today, it is enough to "just not want to drink". The most basic principle of AA is anonymity, no member is required to provide information about his or her identity. A second basic principle of AA is not to receive any external donations but stand its own feet. Members donate for the venues and for the expenses as much as they can afford and nothing is requested from those who cannot. In AA groups, which may be called a kind of solidarity group, the healing rates are higher than the medical interventions and supports. It is said that this ratio has reached 60%.

21. Alexander, B. K., & Hadaway, P. F. (1982). Opiate addiction: The case for an adaptive orientation. Psychological Bulletin, 92(2), 367.

22. Lewis M. (2016). The Biology of Desire: Why Addiction Is Not a Disease. New York: Public Affairs.

23. Steiner A. (2008). Effects of Oxytocin. Lörrach: Cuvillier Verlag

24. Alexander, B. K., Coambs, R. B., & Hadaway, P. F. (1978). "The effect of housing and gender on morphine self-administration in rats." Psychopharmacology, 58(2), 175-179.

25. Kosfeld, M., Heinrichs, M., Zak, P. J., Fischbacher, U., & Fehr, E. (2005). Oxytocin increases trust in humans. Nature, 435(7042), 673-676.

Index

E

F

G

H

I

J

K

L

M

N

O

P

R

CPSIA information can be obtained
at www.ICGtesting.com
Printed in the USA
LVHW111218180721
693014LV00003B/411

9 781973 365341